Ninety Feet Away

The Story of the 2014
Kansas City Royals

by

Kent Krause

Ninety Feet Away

Kodar Publishing
ISBN 13: 978-0-692-40679-3
ISBN 10: 0692406794

For Dad and Mom,

who took me to my first Royals game on June 21, 1976

Other books by Kent Krause:

The All-American King

Men Among Giants

Behind in the Count

Contents

Chapter 1

"We're Back"

He stood alone atop the mound. The surrounding roar amplified into a deafening crescendo that shook the ground beneath his cleats. As ace of the staff, he was the obvious choice to start. Who better to handle the pressure than the man they called Big Game James? Years earlier he had won a World Series game. None of the other starters in the rotation had faced even a single batter in the playoffs. Eight of his nine teammates in the lineup had similarly never experienced postseason action. For them, this was their big game—the biggest game of their careers. After five tense innings, Kansas City nursed a one-run lead over Oakland. It was the 2014 American League Wild Card Game. The winners would advance, the losers would go home. Their season over, with nary a meaningful at-bat in six long months.

Big Game James—aka James Shields—finished his warmup tosses before the sixth inning. A's outfielder Sam Fuld stepped to the plate. Energy pulsed through Kauffman Stadium—more than 40,000 longsuffering fans yelled their support for a team that had not reached the postseason since 1985. The near three-decade span of futility marked the longest playoff drought of any team in the four major American sports.

More than half the Kansas City players had not been born when the Royals last appeared in the postseason. Ronald Reagan

1

occupied the White House. Bill Cosby and J.R. Ewing dominated TV ratings. People listened to music on cassette tapes and vinyl records. The Soviet Union existed. The Internet did not. And phones were not so smart. Spectators taking pictures of the last Royals postseason game did so with cameras that used film rolls that had to be developed—a process that could take hours or even days.

Shields had yielded two runs in the first. Since then, he had cruised along with four shutout innings. The sixth started promisingly for the Kansas City ace when he shattered Fuld's bat with an inside fastball. The resulting blooper, however, dropped into shallow right for a single.

Next up was Josh Donaldson, Oakland's power-hitting third baseman. The batter worked the count full, before taking ball four on a fastball that just missed the outside corner. The A's had runners at first and second with nobody out.

Up in the stands, TBS field reporter Matt Winer interviewed an 87-year-old Kansas City fan named Rich Burstein. A Royals season ticket holder since the team's inception in 1969, Burstein maintained that he knew this day was coming—his confidence not wavering, despite a playoff drought that had spanned one-third of his life. When Winer asked what this day meant for the fans in the stadium, Burstein replied, "*This game ... it's just the reemergence of the Royals. We're back.*"

On the field, meanwhile, Kansas City manager Ned Yost made a critical decision. He removed Big Game James, even though his ace had thrown only 88 pitches. Now tasked with holding the 3-2 lead was Yordano Ventura, a flame-throwing 23-year-old rookie starter who had made just one relief appearance during the season. This pitching change would be the most scrutinized move of the game. Why didn't Yost bring in a southpaw like Danny Duffy or Brandon Finnegan to face the lefty slugger Brandon Moss? Or why not turn to Kelvin Herrera, a fireballing reliever with a 1.41 ERA who specialized in these situations?

The manager had made his decision. Ventura would face Moss, who had crushed a two-run homer off Shields in the first. Though unorthodox, the move offered a reasonable chance for success. Moss had slumped badly in the second half of the season. After August 1st, he had hit just two home runs during a two-month decline that dropped his average to .234. He got lucky once in this game, but surely not again.

Ventura quickly fell behind with two balls. He fired in his third pitch—Moss connected with a mighty swing, launching the fastball over the centerfield wall. When the 432-foot blast landed, the Royals' one-run lead had become a 5-3 deficit. Stunned silence blanketed Kauffman Stadium. The tide had turned.

The next batter, Josh Reddick, lined a single off Ventura. A wild pitch from the rattled hurler sent the runner to second. He moved to third on a sacrifice fly from Jed Lowrie.

Yost trudged to the mound amid a chorus of boos. He took the ball from Ventura and summoned Herrera from the bullpen. Inheriting a difficult situation, the reliever got a huge out by inducing a pop up from Stephen Vogt. With two down, Kansas City could escape with no further damage. Derek Norris, batting next, had other ideas. He singled to drive in Reddick. Two more hits followed to plate the fifth tally of the inning. When the disastrous frame finally ended, the Royals trailed 7-3.

With Kansas City now headed for certain defeat and a quick exit from the postseason, the fans rendered their judgment on who was to blame for this debacle. Yost! With just 12 outs left in the Royals' season, questions about the future already started to materialize. At the top of the list for KC: would their much-maligned skipper survive to manage another year?

WATER OFF A DUCK'S BACK

Thirty-four years earlier Ned Yost debuted as a catcher for Milwaukee in 1980, the same season Royals legend George Brett flirted with .400. The Brewers acquisition of slugging backstop Ted Simmons the following year ensured that Yost would watch most of his team's games from the bench. When Milwaukee reached the 1982 World Series, Yost had one plate appearance—a walk.

In 1983 the Brewers increasingly used Simmons as a designated hitter, allowing Yost more opportunities behind the plate. He caught 61 games for the Crew, but hit just .224. That offseason Milwaukee traded him to Texas for Jim Sundberg. Yost batted .182 for the Rangers, who released him after one season. He signed as a free agent with Montreal in April 1985, but played just five games for the Expos. At age 30, Ned Yost's playing days had ended.

In 1991 Atlanta Braves manager Bobby Cox hired Yost as his bullpen coach. It was a good time to be in Atlanta. During his twelve years coaching for Cox, the Braves reached the World Series five times, including a world championship in 1995.

Following the 2002 season, Milwaukee offered Yost a chance to manage at the big league level. Though a great opportunity for the 47-year-old, the job presented a daunting challenge. The Brewers had finished the previous year with an abysmal 56-106 record—the franchise's tenth consecutive losing season.

Yost looked to be the right man for the job. Not only did he bring a wealth of baseball knowledge from his time with Cox, he had also learned about winning and determination from his longtime friend Dale Earnhardt. When he started managing the Brewers, Yost wore Number 3 as a tribute to the late NASCAR legend. Though it didn't happen overnight, the new skipper righted the ship in Milwaukee. In Yost's third season the Brewers finished 81-81, avoiding a losing record for the first time in 13 years. In 2007 the Crew raced out to an eight-and-a-half-game lead in National League Central. Led by young sluggers Prince Fielder and Ryan Braun, Yost's team brought excitement back to a city that had been lacking in baseball enthusiasm since the early 1990s.

The Brewers, however, faltered in the stretch run. A brutal September allowed the Chicago Cubs to vault ahead, capturing the division by two games. Yost was ejected from four games during the last month, raising questions about whether his combative temperament was hurting the team. Despite the Brewers' recent success, their manager had never gained widespread favor with fans in Wisconsin. Sometimes bristly and defensive in interviews, Yost gained a reputation as an inflexible decision-maker with questionable judgment.

The following season, Milwaukee again surged in the standings, seemingly headed for a playoff spot. But another September swoon threatened to drop the Crew out of the race. Desperate to avoid a second consecutive stretch-run collapse, Milwaukee fired Yost with twelve games left in the season. The team held on to capture the NL Wild Card. Yost retreated to his home in Georgia.

No longer interested in the pennant race, the beleaguered ex-manager did not watch baseball after his firing. Yost instead built feeders for his 700-acre farm and went hunting with his sons and comedian Jeff Foxworthy.

Yost's exile from baseball would not last long. Just a season later, Kansas City general manager Dayton Moore convinced him to accept a consulting position with the Royals. When the team stumbled through the first five weeks of the 2010 season with a 12-23 record, Moore fired skipper Trey Hillman and named Yost the new manager of the Kansas City Royals.

Sailing would not be smooth. As with the Brewers years earlier, he inherited a team with dismal prospects for success. Kansas City had not posted a winning record since 2003. Yost's arrival would not alter this trend—not right away. The team went 55-72 after his hiring to finish 28 games below .500.

More of the same followed in 2011 and 2012 as the Royals continued to hit 90 in the loss column. But in 2013, Yost led the team to a promising 86-76 record. Once again, he had piloted a moribund franchise out of the depths of the second division. While Royals Nation certainly appreciated this upturn in

5

fortunes, they did not shower the manager with accolades. His popularity still paled in comparison with earlier KC skippers Whitey Herzog and Dick Howser.

Even as the team marched to a postseason berth in 2014, fans found much to criticize in Yost's managing style. His handling of pitchers, especially relievers, often defied conventional logic. His affinity for sacrifice bunts seemed outdated and counterproductive in the 21st century game. The manager's head-scratching moves even resulted in the word *yosted* becoming a social media term for poor decision making. While it could be debated whether his surname deserved such an honor, Yost did buck baseball zeitgeist with his persisting preference for "small ball" tactics. Prevailing dugout wisdom instead favored the statistic-driven sabermetric approaches employed by Oakland GM Billy Beane and popularized in the Michael Lewis bestseller, *Moneyball*. In the film adaptation of the book, Brad Pitt played Beane. If a film were made about the Royals, who would play Yost? According to Paul Sullivan of the *Chicago Tribune*, the role would go to Steve Carell for his mastery at portraying bumbling idiots.

Yost's own comments sometimes added to his strained relationship with fans. He ruffled feathers during the season by complaining about low attendance at Royals home games. He even admitted a preference for managing on the road due to the increased pressure of trying to please the fans at home. Nonetheless, Yost maintained the favor of Kansas City's front office. Dayton Moore appreciated his manager's competitive nature, describing Yost as "an incredible leader and very passionate."

In 2014 Yost defied his inflexible reputation by applying some of the lessons learned from his many years in the dugout. One of which was to loosen the reins on his players. "They play hard for each other," the manager said. "Just letting them be themselves. It was a big lesson I learned." His team appreciated the new hands-off style of allowing players greater autonomy. First baseman Eric Hosmer voiced this approval of the new

Yost. "He's changed along with the players, and we all really respect and appreciate that."

Indeed, Yost's players remained his staunchest defenders. Taking issue with the many criticisms of his manager, pitcher Wade Davis pointed out, "A lot more of his decisions turn out to be right than wrong." Danny Duffy added that Yost "always has your back, always." Catcher Salvador Perez concurred: "He loves us like we were his own children, and you want to play hard for someone like that."

But did the criticism and lack of respect in the sports pages and blogs ever bother Yost? Described by Moore as "thick-skinned," the manager maintained that it did not. Commenting on his status as a punching bag, Yost said, "When people boo me or say bad things about me, it's just water off a duck's back."

A SEASON SLIPPING AWAY

While the boos raining down on him in the sixth inning of the Wild Card Game may not have bothered Yost, the score certainly did. His Royals trailed 7-3 against Oakland's Jon Lester, a top-of-the-rotation ace who thrived in the postseason. Billy Beane had traded away one of baseball's best young sluggers, Yoenis Cespedes, to acquire Lester in a midseason deal with Boston. Given Lester's 4-1 record the previous postseason for the Red Sox, including two wins in the World Series, Oakland appeared to have the right man on the mound for this "win-or-go-home" contest. Especially considering that Lester had owned the Royals, shackling them with a 1.84 ERA in 13 career starts against Kansas City.

Lester sent the Royals down in order in the bottom of the sixth. Kansas City managed a bunt single in the seventh, but again did not score. Oakland maintained its four-run lead and now needed just six outs to finish off the home team. At this point in the game, the A's win probability stood at 96%.

Alcides Escobar led off the bottom of the eighth. The Royals infielder sent a chopper up the middle that barely eluded the glove of Oakland shortstop Jed Lowrie for a base hit. With the next batter, Nori Aoki, at the plate, Escobar stole second. Devotees of sabermetrics frown upon sending runners in such situations. The risk is too great. If Escobar had been caught, the Royals would have squandered what little opportunity they had to get back in this game. According to modern statistical experts, teams should attempt fewer steals.

Ned Yost's Royals led the majors with 153 stolen bases in the regular season.

Aoki hit a sharp grounder to second. Though Oakland retired Aoki at first, the runner advanced to third. Escobar's theft had saved his team from a double play, but now the Royals teetered only five outs from elimination.

Kansas City centerfielder Lorenzo Cain stepped into the batter's box to face Lester. The situation remained dire. But as they did in 1985, Royals fans refused to surrender even when their heroes faced near-hopeless circumstances on the field. With Kansas City's season slipping away, the crowd at Kauffman Stadium broke into a familiar rallying cry: "Let's go Royals … Let's go Royals …"

Chapter 2

Glory Seasons

Even if Yost's boys fell in the AL Wild Card Game, as it seemed certain they would do, the 2014 Royals had already made history. As Rich Burstein pointed out, just by claiming a Wild Card spot the team had revived a rich baseball tradition in Kansas City.

Major league baseball in KC dated back to the nineteenth century when the city fielded teams that played in the Union Association, the American Association, and the National League. While these clubs had little success during their brief existences, the 1889 Kansas City Cowboys did feature a future Hall of Famer in "Sliding" Billy Hamilton, whose 914 career stolen bases would stand as the MLB record for eight decades.

KC sports fans went without big league baseball from 1890 until 1914, when the Federal League emerged to challenge the two major leagues of Organized Baseball. The Kansas City Packers struggled during their first season, but rebounded in 1915 to finish in fourth place with an 81-72 record. The Federal League folded after just its second season, however, leaving Kansas City again without a major league team.

The 1920s marked a baseball renaissance in Kansas City with the establishment of a Negro League franchise in town. Founded by sports executive J.L. Wilkinson, the Kansas City Monarchs won the first Negro League World Series in 1924. The team won eleven league championships in the span of three decades. Pitcher Satchel Paige became the Monarch's top draw in the 1940s, helping Kansas City prevail in the 1942 Negro League World Series over the Homestead Grays. Jackie Robinson, Ernie Banks, Cool Papa Bell, and Buck O'Neil were among the many star players who wore a Monarchs uniform.

The return of major league baseball to Kansas City in the 1950s marked the end of the Monarchs' run as the city's top diamond attraction. In 1955 industrialist Arnold Johnson moved his newly-acquired Philadelphia Athletics franchise to Kansas City. Enthusiasm for baseball swelled in the region, with the team drawing nearly 1.4 million spectators during its first season—a total the Athletics had never approached in Philly.

The Kansas City Athletics won their 1955 home opener over Detroit by a score of 6-2. After that, things went downhill for pretty much the next thirteen seasons. The Athletics routinely lost 90-plus games and never finished higher than sixth place. The franchise became best known as an unofficial farm team of the New York Yankees. Roger Maris, Ralph Terry, Ryne Duren, Enos Slaughter, and Bobby Shantz were among the Athletics sent east to help the Bronx Bombers remain atop the American League.

Team fortunes somehow worsened after Charley O. Finley acquired the franchise in 1960. Though he livened up the uniforms to kelly green and bright gold, the new owner ruled with a heavy hand, frequently berating his players and managers in public. To draw fans Finley employed several outside-the-box gimmicks, such as a sheep herd grazing beyond the outfield wall, a mule mascot named Charlie O, and a mechanical rabbit that popped out of the ground to present baseballs to the umpire. Perhaps the best promotion came in 1965 when 59-year-old mound legend Satchell Paige appeared in a game for the Athletics. Pitching three scoreless innings, Paige became the oldest player ever to compete in a major league baseball game.

Despite Finley's unconventional ideas, the losing continued and attendance dwindled. After the 1967 season, Finley gained permission from the league to move his team to Oakland. Missouri U.S. Senator Stuart Symington summarized the views of many Kansas Citians when he called Finley "one of the most disreputable characters ever to enter the American sports scene."

BUILDING A CONTENDER

Though not heartbroken to see Finley's A's depart, Kansas City fans, including Symington, refused to accept the absence of big league baseball from their town. Motivated by the senator's threats to instigate congressional action against baseball's antitrust exemption, American League officials moved quickly to return baseball to KC. In 1969 MLB would place expansion franchises in Kansas City and Seattle. The American League accepted the bid of pharmaceutical giant Ewing Kauffman to become the new owner of the Kansas City team, nicknamed the Royals as a nod to the American Royal livestock show held in the city since 1899.

In one of his first moves, Kauffman hired Cedric Tallis as the team's general manager. A longtime executive for the Los Angeles Angels, Tallis brought two decades of front office experience to the Royals. Kauffman's choice turned out to be a gift that would keep on giving for many years.

Similar to the Monarchs and Athletics, the new franchise played its home games at Municipal Stadium at East 22nd Street and Brooklyn Avenue. The Royals won their first game in a come-from-behind twelve-inning victory over Minnesota. But, as expansion teams tend to do, the 1969 Royals lost much more than they won. Lou Piniella captured the Rookie of the Year Award, but the team dropped 93 games under manager Joe Gordon.

Following a dismal sophomore season, the Royals surprised the baseball world by posting an 85-76 record in 1971. In only its third year in existence, Kauffman's team had already logged the winningest major league campaign in Kansas City's history. Regression set in the next season, unfortunately, resulting in another losing record. Kauffman responded by sacking popular manager Bob Lemon and replacing him with Jack McKeon.

The 1973 season brought the excitement of a new home—Royals Stadium at the Harry S. Truman Sports Complex. The beautiful ballpark featured a twelve-story "crown" scoreboard and multicolored fountains in the outfield. This state-of-the-art venue helped draw a franchise record 1,345,341 fans that year. The team responded with its best campaign to date: 88 wins and a second-place finish in the American League West.

Throughout these early years, Tallis engineered a series of one-sided trades to bolster the Kansas City roster. Among the future stars netted in these shrewd deals were Amos Otis, Cookie Rojas, Freddie Patek, John Mayberry, and Hal McRae. In addition to Tallis's annual plundering of opposing rosters, the team established a baseball academy to find and develop new talent. This controversial brainchild of Kauffman lasted only five years, but delivered to the parent club perennial Gold Glove winner Frank White and U.L. Washington.

Despite an impressive assemblage of talent, the 1974 Royals dropped to fifth in the standings. Dissension festered within the organization. Kauffman fired his star GM Tallis. When the team struggled in the first half of the 1975 season, Kauffman lowered the axe on his manager too. To replace McKeon, the Royals hired Whitey Herzog, a former Texas manager who had once played infield for the Kansas City Athletics. The new skipper rallied the team to a 41-25 finish to close within seven games of the A's for the division title. Despite the early-season turmoil, at 91-71 Kansas City had recorded its most successful season to date.

Herzog arrived in town at an opportune time. The team's farm system, much blessed by the work of Art Stewart and other keen-eyed scouts, was yielding a crop of talented players. Ace right-hander Steve Busby won 56 games from 1973 to 1975, tossing two no-hitters in that span. Paul Splittorff and Dennis Leonard had also emerged in the Kansas City rotation. Frank

White was showing promise as a middle infielder and the team had a kid at third base with some potential.

Drafted as a shortstop in 1971, George Brett steadily advanced through the Royals farm system. In 1973 he batted .284 in Omaha with 117 RBI. Winning the third baseman job for Kansas City the following year, Brett became a devoted student of team hitting instructor Charlie Lau. Rigorously applying Lau's precepts, Brett led the AL in hits in 1975, just his second full season in the majors. Emulating teammate Hal McRae's aggressive baserunning, Brett also tied for the lead in triples. And Number 5 was just getting started.

YEARS OF TRIUMPH AND HEARTBREAK

After six years of savvy trades and visionary draft picks, Kansas City boasted one of the most talented rosters in baseball. With the addition of Whitey Herzog's baseball knowledge and competitive spirit, many predicted the Royals would soar to new heights in 1976. Standing in their way, however, were the Oakland A's. Since leaving Kansas City, Charlie Finley's team had won three World Series and five straight AL West titles. To Kansas City fans, baseball had no larger villain than Finley.

Following a slow start in April, the Royals caught fire in May, winning 16 out of 19 to grab the division lead. Kansas City built its cushion over Oakland to a comfortable 12 games by early August. But the A's chipped away at the lead, aided by a disastrous stretch in which Kansas City lost nine of ten. On September 28th, the Royals' division lead had shriveled to two and a half games. And the team had one more showdown in Oakland. Having lost Busby to injury earlier that summer, Herzog sent the unheralded Larry Gura to the mound. The southpaw reliever had started only one game the entire season. Brett and his teammates wondered if their skipper had lost his mind.

With legions of fans across the Heartland hanging on the play-by-play descriptions from Royals radio announcers Fred

White and Denny Matthews, Gura pitched a crucial four-hit shutout to lower the team's magic number to one. Two nights later the A's lost at California, giving Kansas City its first AL West title. The Royals were headed to the playoffs.

Awaiting Kansas City in the American League Championship Series were the New York Yankees, led by fiery manager Billy Martin. After dominating baseball by winning 20 world championships and 29 pennants from 1921 to 1964, the Bronx Bombers had hit a dry spell. The team had not reached the postseason in twelve years. The glory days of Ruth, DiMaggio and Mantle seemed like ancient history to Yankee fans starved for a pennant.

The ALCS opened at Royals Stadium. Aided by two Brett errors, the Yankees scored twice in the first inning of Game 1. The Royals never recovered, eventually losing 4-1. Making matters worse, Amos Otis suffered an ankle injury that ended the star centerfielder's season. Despite this setback, Kansas City evened the series by capturing Game 2. The pattern continued in New York with the Yankees winning Game 3 and the Royals taking Game 4.

In the pennant-deciding contest, John Mayberry put the Royals up early with a two-run homer in the top of the first. The Yankees quickly tied it and pulled ahead with two scores in the third. After seven innings, New York had increased its lead to 6-3. The Royals season appeared to be over. But with one dramatic swing, Brett clubbed a three-run homer in the eighth to tie the game.

As the Bronx crowd fell silent, elation and renewed hope swept through the multitude of Royals fans watching the action on television or listening on their radios. Sadly, this joy would prove ephemeral. Chris Chambliss led off the Yankee ninth with a drive that barely cleared the right field wall. New York advanced to the World Series, while Kansas City slunk home with a gut-wrenching loss.

The Royals entered 1977 with a loaded roster and unprecedented confidence. After losing the pennant by one run the previous October, the players were determined to break though. Two months into the season, however, the team languished below .500. By mid-June, the Royals fell seven games behind in the division. Then, as the summer got hotter, so too did the Royals. An eight-game July winning streak pulled KC within two games of the division lead. In August the Royals reeled off ten straight wins to vault to the top of the AL West. And Whitey's boys were not finished. Like Secretariat at the Belmont Stakes, the Royals accelerated in the stretch run—winning an astonishing 24 of 25 games—to easily claim the division. The historic string of wins propelled Kansas City to a 102-60 record, a franchise mark that still stands.

Though he later won three NL pennants with the Cardinals, Whitey Herzog called the 1977 Royals the best team he ever managed. Indeed, the Royals had hitting: six players drove in more than 75 runs, including 112 RBI from Al Cowens; the Royals had power: four players hit 20-plus home runs; the Royals had speed: six players reached double digits in stolen bases, paced by Freddie Patek's league-leading 53. And finally, the Royals had pitching: Dennis Leonard led the starters with 20 wins and 244 strikeouts. Jim Colborn won 18 games, including a no-hitter. Paul Splittorff topped the AL in winning percentage with a 16-6 mark.

Again facing New York in the playoffs, Kansas City took two of the first three games. Needing to win just one of the next two contests, both at Royals Stadium, Whitey's boys had the pennant within their grasp. But in Game 4, first baseman John Mayberry showed up in a daze after partying late with relatives the night before. He dropped two throws and a foul pop, and twice struck out. Herzog replaced him in the fifth with John Wathan, but Kansas City could not overcome Mickey Rivers's four hits and Sparky Lyle's five-plus scoreless relief innings. New York prevailed 6-4.

Taking the hill for the decisive Game 5, Splittorff allowed only one run through seven innings. The Royals led 3-2 heading into the ninth. Needing just three outs for the pennant, Herzog called on Leonard to preserve the one-run lead. Given that the right-hander had thrown a complete game only two days earlier, and had made just one relief appearance that season, this move would provoke an avalanche of second-guessing.

Yankee outfielder Paul Blair fell behind in the count 1-2, before looping a single into center. And so began the worst nightmare inning in Royals history. A walk put runners at first and second. Gura replaced Leonard and surrendered a single to Mickey Rivers that drove in the tying run. With the season slipping away, Herzog summoned Mark Littell, who allowed a sacrifice fly that put New York ahead. A throwing error by Brett gave the Yankees another run. The Royals dominating season ended with a crushing 5-3 defeat.

Hal McRae considered the playoff loss his biggest disappointment in baseball. His teammates concurred. "It was the worst defeat ever for me," said Frank White, "and I'm talking about every game I'd played since Little League." Calling the 1977 team the best in franchise history, Brett expressed similar feelings. "We had it and we gave it away," the third baseman said. "It's never stopped hurting."

A bitter Herzog forced the team to send Mayberry packing. Otherwise the 1978 Royals featured much of the same cast from the previous year. Leonard, Splittorff, and Gura combined for 56 wins and Kansas City again captured the AL West.

And Kansas City again faced the Yankees in the ALCS. Following a familiar script, the teams split the first two games at Royals Stadium. Brett hit three home runs in Game 3 to give Kansas City a one-run lead heading into the bottom of the eighth. Waiting in the bullpen was "The Mad Hungarian" Al Hrabowsky, who had saved 20 games for the Royals during the regular season. Herzog instead summoned Doug Bird and his

5.29 ERA. Yankee catcher Thurman Munson blasted a mammoth two-run homer off Bird. The Yankees won 6-5.

The following night, New York finished off the Royals behind Ron Guidry's lights out pitching. Three straight seasons Kansas City had lost in the playoffs to the Yankees. And in all three series, the Royals bullpen gave up late-inning runs to lose crucial games.

Believing that Ewing Kauffman and his wife Muriel did not like him, Whitey Herzog predicted he would be fired if the Royals ever failed to win their division. Despite big offensive years from Brett, outfielder Willie Wilson, and catcher Darrell Porter, Kansas City finished second in the AL West in 1979, three games behind California. The prescient Herzog was fired.

General Manager Joe Burke maintained that it was more than just personal feelings that resulted in the move. He believed the skipper had repeatedly put the team in impossible situations. Others criticized Whitey for trying to make himself bigger than the organization. His questionable pitching moves in the playoffs did not help matters. The manager's support among the players, moreover, had diminished after he shipped off Mayberry and fired the popular hitting coach Charlie Lau.

Herzog had taken the Royals to new heights, but the team plateaued and management believed "the White Rat" could elevate them no further. If Kansas City was going to reach the next level, it would be with someone else at the helm.

VANQUISHING THE EVIL EMPIRE

The Royals hired longtime Baltimore coach Jim Frey to lead the team into the 1980s. While the core of Herzog's division winners remained in place, this edition of the Royals featured several new pieces. Burke traded Cowens to California for power-hitting first baseman Willie Aikens. Switch-hitting Academy graduate U.L. Washington (and his toothpick) replaced Patek at shortstop. And submariner Dan Quisenberry gave Frey a legitimate closer in the bullpen.

After starting slow in 1980, the Royals again heated up with the rising temperatures of late spring. The team moved into first place on May 23rd and never looked back. Paced by Leonard (20 wins), Gura (18 wins), and Splittorff (14 wins), Kansas City built its lead to 20 games by the end of August and cruised to another division title.

Wilson turned in a stellar season, hitting .326 and stealing 79 bases, while setting a then-MLB record with 705 at-bats. Wathan, Aikens, and McRae also produced at the plate, but it was George Brett who grabbed national headlines that summer of 1980. Slashing hit after hit, the star third baseman made a run at .400, a mark that had not been reached since 1941. Though hampered by injuries, Brett finished the season with a .390 average, 24 homers, and 118 RBI—numbers that earned him the AL MVP.

Again looming in the ALCS, however, were the New York Yankees and their major league-leading 103 wins. Undaunted, Gura and Leonard pitched KC to victory in the first two games. Never before had the Royals reached this position. The team arrived in New York needing to take just one game out of three.

Red hot Frank White homered to give Kansas City a fifth-inning lead in Game 3. But when New York pulled ahead 2-1 in the bottom of the sixth, Royals fans wondered if yet another playoff series was starting to slip away. With two outs in the top of the seventh, Wilson doubled off Tommy John. Yankee skipper Dick Howser summoned the flame-throwing Goose Gossage. Firing bullets that reached the high 90s, the nearly unhittable closer had posted a 2.27 ERA during the season. Battling Gossage to a full count, U.L. Washington chopped a ball up the middle that he barely beat out for an infield hit. The Royals had runners at the corners with Number 5 stepping to the plate.

Casting aside past playoff demons, Brett launched Goose's first offering into the upper deck of Yankee Stadium. While New York owner George Steinbrenner fumed, the crowd sat in stunned silence. "We were going crazy in the dugout," Frank

White said, "and as George ran the bases, there wasn't a sound from the stands. It was so sweet." Quisenberry pitched three and two-thirds innings of scoreless relief to preserve the 4-2 lead. At last the Royals had won the pennant. And they did it in the Bronx, against their perennial tormenters.

Riding a huge wave of momentum, the Royals arrived in Philadelphia to open the 1980 World Series against the Phillies. Two-run homers from Otis and Aikens gave KC an early 4-0 lead in Game 1. But Philadelphia struck back for five runs against Leonard in the bottom of the third. The Royals fell 7-6.

The next day, Philadelphia rocked Quisenberry with four runs in the eighth to take Game 2. Brett, meanwhile, made headlines when he removed himself from the game due to a severe pain in his posterior. During the off-day, he underwent minor surgery to remove hemorrhoids. As he later assessed, "My ailment will go down in the anals of World Series history."

With his problems behind him, Brett homered to help Kansas City win Game 3. Aikens hit two more home runs in Game 4 to fuel another KC victory. With the Series tied, the Royals took a one-run lead into the ninth inning of Game 5. But once again, the Phillies tagged Quisenberry with a heartbreaking loss. Philadelphia ace Steve Carlton shut down the Royals in Game 6 to close out the Series.

It was a familiar story for Kansas City—a season filled with exciting performances and dramatic victories ended with disappointment. Questions lingered: How did a team with the league-leader in saves blow two late-inning leads? How did Wilson, who led the league with 230 hits, strike out twelve times against the Phillies? And why did the world's most famous case of hemorrhoids have to strike when it did?

REACHING THE SUMMIT

The players' strike divided the 1981 campaign into two mini-seasons. After the Royals played poorly in the first half and started the second half with similar mediocrity, Burke axed Jim

Frey and replaced him with former Yankee skipper Dick Howser. The new manager rekindled the team's fire, leading them to a first-place finish in the second mini-season. But Billy Martin's Oakland A's swept Kansas City in the first round of the playoffs.

In 1982 Whitey Herzog led his new team, the St. Louis Cardinals, to the world championship. His former team in Kansas City, meanwhile, missed the playoffs for only the second time in seven seasons. The Royals again missed the playoffs in 1983, finishing 20 games behind the Chicago White Sox. For Kansas City the season is most remembered for George Brett's infamous "Pine Tar" game and the federal indictment of Willie Wilson, Willie Aikens, Vida Blue, and Jerry Martin. All four pleaded guilty to drug possession and served short prison sentences. Only Wilson would return to the Royals.

Howser's boys rebounded in 1984 to win a weak American League West. But their return to postseason play ended quickly when Sparky Anderson's Detroit juggernaut swept KC in the ALCS. Of greater significance, however, were the roster moves the Royals had been making.

John Schuerholz, promoted to GM three years earlier, returned to a time-tested Royals strategy of making shrewd trades and developing young talent in the farm system. In deals reminiscent of Tallis a decade earlier, Schuerholz acquired southpaw Charlie Leibrandt from the Reds, slugger Steve Balboni from the Yankees, and veteran catcher Jim Sundberg from the Brewers. Early in the 1985 season, Schuerholz filched speedy outfielder Lonnie Smith from the Cardinals. From the farm, the Royals had promoted in '84 the promising pitching trio of Bret Saberhagen, Danny Jackson, and Mark Gubicza. These newcomers joined KC's seasoned veterans Brett, White, Wilson, McRae, Wathan, and Quisenberry.

To say the 1985 Royals did not do anything easily is perhaps the biggest understatement in franchise history. Streaky and mediocre play left the Royals 7.5 games behind the Angels on July 21. With little more than two months remaining in the season, postseason hopes faded. The team then reeled off a seven-game winning streak to claw back into the race. With a 13-2 run in September, Kansas City vaulted into first with just two weeks to go. But the Royals proceeded to drop four straight at home to the hapless Mariners. A week later Minnesota swept Howser's boys in the Metrodome. Kansas City trailed California by one game with five left to play.

With the season on the line, lefty Bud Black shut out the Angels to move his team into a tie for the division lead. Danny Jackson bested California the next night to push Kansas City into first. On the final weekend of the season, the Royals took two of three from Oakland to secure the division title.

Opposing Kansas City in the ALCS were Bobby Cox's Toronto Blue Jays, winners of 99 games (eight more than the Royals) during the regular season. After Toronto ace Dave Stieb shut down Kansas City in Game 1, sloppy play cost the Royals a late lead in Game 2. Returning home in a two-game hole, Brett unleashed a four-hit barrage, including two homers and four runs scored, to propel his team to a 6-5 victory. Leibrandt pitched eight shutout innings in Game 4, but Toronto scored three runs in the ninth to bury KC with a crushing loss.

Facing a disheartening 3-1 series deficit, Danny Jackson weaved a shutout in Game 5 to stave off elimination. Back in Toronto, Gubicza, Black, and Quisenberry yielded just three runs, while Brett drilled a go-ahead homer, to tie the series at three games apiece. An already tense Game 7 grew tighter when a comebacker forced Saberhagen from the mound with a swollen hand after just three innings. Leibrandt took over and kept the Blue Jays in check. Batting in the sixth with the bases loaded, Sundberg launched a triple off the top of the right field fence to break open a one-run game. Three innings later, Kansas City was heading to its second World Series.

Waiting to face the Royals was the team on the other side of Missouri—Whitey Herzog's St. Louis Cardinals, winners of 101 games. Unfortunately for the Royals, the I-70 Series started just like the ALCS when Cardinal ace John Tudor shut them down in Game 1. The following night, the Royals blew a two-run lead in the ninth to waste a stellar outing from Leibrandt and drop Game 2. Much like Ned Yost three decades later, Howser faced a firestorm of criticism for his pitching decisions—in this case failing to replace his tired starter in the ninth.

Unlikely cleanup hitter Frank White provided the power in Game 3 as Saberhagen pitched the Royals to victory. Tudor, however, followed with a dominating five-hit shutout to claim Game 4 for the Cardinals. Once again, Kansas City found itself buried in a three-games-to-one series deficit. And once again, Danny Jackson responded with a much-needed complete game victory to stave off elimination for the Royals.

The Series returned to Kansas City for Game 6. Leibrandt battled Danny Cox in a tense pitchers' duel. In the eighth, St. Louis blooped home a run to break a scoreless tie. Leibrandt once again appeared destined for a tough late-inning loss. With the Royals trailing 1-0 heading into the bottom of the ninth, Cardinal fireballer Todd Worrell took the mound to get the final three outs needed to wrap up the World Series. Pinch hitter Jorge Orta led off with a bouncer that first baseman Jack Clark fielded and tossed to Worrell for the out ... until umpire Don Denkinger called him safe. Replays confirmed that the throw beat Orta. Herzog and the Cardinals vigorously argued, but in 1985 managers could not call for a video challenge. The umpire's call stood—Orta remained on first with nobody out.

Steve Balboni hit a foul pop that Clark failed to catch. With new life, the Royals slugger grounded a single into left. After Sundberg bunted into a force out, the Royals had runners at first and second with one down. With his former teammate McRae batting, St. Louis catcher Darrell Porter allowed a passed ball to advance the runners. Herzog ordered Worrell to walk McRae and load the bases. Former Cardinals World Series hero Dane Iorg stepped to the plate. Swinging at a 1-0 fastball, Iorg looped a single to right. One run scored and Sundberg rounded third, sliding home just ahead of Porter's tag. The Royals won 2-1, tying the series at three games apiece.

The Cardinals arrived at the ballpark for Game 7 embittered and shell-shocked. Kansas City's lineup pounded their ace Tudor and six other pitchers for 11 runs. Saberhagen meanwhile tossed a masterful five-hit shutout. The team that had suffered so much postseason heartbreak had won an unprecedented six elimination games. The Kansas City Royals were world champions.

As George Brett later said, "Even when your grandkids have grandkids, nobody will win it the way we did in eighty-five."

The 1888 Kansas City Cowboys finished last in the American Association with a 43-89 record. Henry Porter (top left) started 54 games and pitched 474 innings.

Kansas City's first major league star, Billy Hamilton batted .301 and scored 144 runs for the Cowboys in 1889. After the franchise dissolved the following year, Hamilton played 12 seasons in the NL for Philadelphia and Boston. The top base runner of his day, he retired in 1901 with a .344 lifetime batting average.
Library of Congress

The Kansas City Monarchs defeated Hilldale in the first Negro League World Series in 1924.
Library of Congress

24

The Kansas City Athletics host the New York Yankees at Municipal Stadium in 1966.
Missouri State Archives

Royals owner Ewing Kauffman and executive vice president Cedric Tallis
in 1968. *Missouri State Archives*

Right fielder Tom Poquette bats against the White Sox at Royals Stadium in 1976. Kansas City went on to win the AL West that year, making its first ever playoff appearance.
Missouri State Archives

Manager Dick Howser presents President Ronald Reagan with a Royals hat, jacket, and bat during a ceremony honoring the 1985 world champions at the White House Rose Garden. *National Archives and Records Administration*

After 21 seasons with the Royals, George Brett retired with a .305 avg., 3,154 hits, 317 homers, and 1,596 RBI. In 1985 he batted .335 with 30 HRs, 112 RBI and a Gold Glove to help Kansas City win the world championship. Brett was inducted into the National Baseball Hall of Fame in 1999.
Missouri State Archives

Mark Gubicza with his teammates in the dugout at Royals Stadium. The right-hander won 132 games for Kansas City from 1984 to 1996.
Missouri State Archives

Chapter 3

Decades of Drought

Following the championship season, Royals fans had many reasons to be optimistic about their team's future prospects. Cy Young winner Bret Saberhagen headed a formidable rotation that included Charlie Leibrandt, Mark Gubicza, and Danny Jackson. Closer Dan Quisenberry had led the AL in saves four straight years. On the offensive side, George Brett still reigned as one of the best hitters in the game. Veterans Frank White, Hal McRae, and Willie Wilson also remained productive. And in the dugout, cool-thinking Dick Howser knew how to get the best out of his players.

Kansas City furthermore had history on its side. The team had reached the playoffs seven of the previous ten seasons. And this trend appeared likely to continue for years to come. The only question was how many more flags would be flying above Royals Stadium by the end of the decade?

In April 1986, mound workhorse Dennis Leonard returned from a two-year rehabilitation absence to pitch a three-hit shutout. The Royals rotation became even more formidable. But the momentum would not last. Injuries slowed Jackson, Gubicza and Saberhagen, who posted a mediocre 7-12, 4.15 ERA, in '86. Brett missed nearly a quarter of the season, while slumping to .290 with just 73 RBI.

The most devastating blow came in July when doctors diagnosed Dick Howser with a malignant brain tumor. The beloved manager had to take a leave of absence and the reeling team limped to the finish line with a losing record.

Howser tried to return for the 1987 season, but surgeries and radiation had left him too weak. Billy Gardner took over as skipper of a team determined to rebound. Kansas City added slugging outfielder Danny Tartabull (34 HRs, 101 RBI), third baseman Kevin Seitzer (207 hits) and perhaps the world's greatest athlete in Bo Jackson. Saberhagen and Leibrandt returned to form, combining for 34 wins.

Though devastated by Howser's death on June 17th, the team remained competitive. A four-game sweep of Toronto pulled KC into a tie for first on July 5th. But the Royals fell into a 4-17 tailspin that dropped them below .500. Management fired Gardner in August, replacing him with John Wathan. A member of Kansas City's glory teams of the '70s and '80s, the new skipper tried to rally the troops. The Royals won nine of their last eleven, but finished two games shy of catching Minnesota for the AL West title.

Unfortunately for Wathan, he would be trying to lead the Royals back at the same time a baseball juggernaut emerged in the same division. Tony La Russa's Oakland A's averaged 102 wins a season from 1988 to 1990, while capturing three straight AL West titles. Kansas City's best chance came in 1989. Powered by another Cy Young season from Saberhagen and 105 RBI from Bo Jackson, Wathan's boys remained in the race into September. Their 92 wins actually topped the team's total from 1985, but still fell short of the dominant A's.

Making matters worse, the acumen of KC's front office started to decline. Deviating from the formula that had worked so well in the past, Schuerholz started rolling the dice on high-priced free agents, most notably closer Mark Davis. Money not well spent. Schuerholz also made what he later called his worst trade ever by sending pitching prospect David Cone to the Mets for catcher Ed Hearn. Hearn contributed little as a backup, while

Cone went 20-3 for New York in 1988, the first of many brilliant seasons for the right-hander. That same year Danny Jackson, whom Schuerholz had traded to the Reds, won 23 games and finished second in the NL Cy Young voting. Though the Royals did acquire a decent shortstop in Kurt Stillwell and future closer Jeff Montgomery in the 1987-88 offseason, much had changed since Tallis's one-sided raids on opposing rosters.

Kansas City dropped to sixth place in 1990. One of the year's few bright spots came when 37-year-old Brett won another batting title—the only player to accomplish the feat in three different decades. After the season, the team cut loose the popular mainstays Frank White and Willie Wilson. More bad news came in January 1991 when Bo Jackson sustained a severe hip injury while pursuing his football "hobby." He would never again play for the Royals.

Another significant loss followed when John Schuerholz decided to leave Kansas City for Atlanta. His missteps of the late 1980s notwithstanding, Schuerholz had been a major architect of the Royals' past triumphs. His departure weakened the KC front office. After Schuerholz arrived in Georgia, the Braves won fourteen straight division titles, five NL pennants, and one World Series. As for Kansas City ... let's just say the team had less success over that span.

As high-priced free agent acquisitions Storm Davis, Mark Davis, and Kirk Gibson floundered, the 1991 Royals languished in sixth place. After the season, GM Herk Robinson shocked fans by trading Saberhagen to the Mets. Also gone was Wathan, whom management had replaced with Hal McRae. Despite the new skipper's efforts, Kansas City finished an abysmal 18 games below .500 in '92. The season's lone highlight came in September when Brett joined the 3,000-hit club.

The pitching of emerging ace Kevin Appier (18-8), returning David Cone (3.33 ERA), and reliever Jeff Montgomery (45 saves) revived Kansas City's fortunes in 1993. The offense improved as well with solid campaigns from Mike Macfarlane, Wally Joyner, Greg Gagne, and the manager's son

Brian McRae. Brett contributed 19 homers and 75 RBI in his final season. The team finished with an encouraging 84-78 mark.

In 1994 slugging first baseman Bob "the Hammer" Hamelin added to a potent lineup. Hamelin's power totals earned him the Rookie of the Year Award, while Cone's mound excellence brought home the Cy Young Award. Reminiscent of KC's glory days, McRae's boys went on a 14-game winning streak that summer. When the players' strike ended play in August, the Royals were 13 games over .500 and only four games out of first in the AL Central (realignment had moved the team from the AL West). The work stoppage, however, wiped out the '94 playoffs and the World Series, thereby eliminating the team's best chance for postseason baseball in nearly a decade.

INTO THE ABYSS

Despite Kansas City's mini-revival, Robinson fired McRae in the offseason. The GM said the team was getting younger and needed a manager who could better relate to up-and-coming players. Not helping McRae's job security was his tendency to alienate fans and reporters with surly comments. Perhaps his most memorable moment as skipper was his profanity-laced postgame tirade in April 1993, complete with a flying phone and an eloquent closing line about pipe smoking.

Former Royal Bob Boone replaced McRae in the KC dugout. Also new for the 1995 season, the ballpark featured grass instead of artificial turf. The changes did not help. Kansas City finished below .500 and 30 games behind the division-winning Cleveland Indians. And so began a string of dismal losing seasons for the Boys in Blue. After a fifth-place finish in 1996, Robinson fired Boone midway through the '97 season in favor of Tony Muser.

The change in skippers did nothing to revive the team's fortunes. Kansas City never finished better than eight games below .500 during the Muser era, which ended with his axing during the 2002 season. In all fairness though, poor managing was not the reason for the downturn. Things had changed higher up. This was not your father's Kansas City front office.

Team president Joe Burke died in May 1992. The following year, owner Ewing Kauffman died on August 1st—just a month after the team renamed the stadium in his honor. In September 1993, Walmart CEO David Glass was appointed Chair of the Royals Board of Directors. The Board controlled franchise operations until Glass bought the team in April 2000 for $96 million.

Under Glass's direction—as chair and later as owner—the Royals followed the Walmart model of minimizing operating costs. The Board reduced the team's budget for player compensation. Kansas City would no longer pay to keep successful veterans receiving high salaries. Cutting operating expenses also meant spending less money on the amateur draft and developing young talent. While other franchises stepped up their investments in the burgeoning gold mine of Latin America, Kansas City fell behind in that crucial arena.

Compounding the problem was a lack of income for the small market Royals. In 1985 Kansas City drew nearly 2.2 million fans, fifth best in the American League. For the 2002 season, the team barely reached 1.3 million, second lowest in the AL. Not surprisingly, the team's ticket and television revenues were among the lowest in baseball. And no longer could the Royals fall back on the bankroll of Kauffman or his 1980s co-owner Avron Fogelman.

Declining revenues and a leadership committed to running the team like a discount department store did not bode well for putting a contender on the field. Fans grew frustrated watching promising young players rise up through the farm system, only to take their talents elsewhere as they hit their prime. Through the bleak 1990s and early 2000s, Kansas City still featured exciting players like Johnny Damon, Jermaine Dye, and Carlos Beltran. But as these players approached free agent eligibility and could command larger salaries, the budget-conscious Board traded them away.

Mike Sweeney was the exception. Drafted by prescient Royals scouting director Art Stewart, the slugging first baseman emerged as a star in the late 1990s. In 2000 he drove in 144 runs, setting a team record that still stands. Labeling him the face of the franchise, management paid $11 million a year to keep Sweeney in Kansas City. And he nearly led the team back to the postseason.

Fueled by offensive production from Sweeney, Raul Ibanez, and Joe Randa, the Royals burst out of the gate with nine straight wins to start the 2003 season. New manager Tony Pena inspired the team to play with a fire and intensity that had been lacking for years. Kansas City surged to the top of the AL Central, building its lead to 7.5 games by mid-July. Fans flocked to the ballpark, increasing total attendance by a half-million over the previous season.

Kansas City maintained its lead in the AL Central through late August. But Royals pitching did not hold up, and Pena's boys faded over the final month. Kansas City finished 83-79. The team posted its first winning record in nine years, but fell seven games short of the division-winning Twins.

In the aftermath of the most exciting season in a decade, KC fans wondered: *Is Royals baseball finally back?*

Sadly, the answer was no. A resounding no. The kind of *no* that follows when the Dungeons & Dragons-playing, *Star Trek*-quoting chess club president asks the homecoming queen for a date. NO!!!

The 2004 Royals flopped to an astonishing 104 losses. That set a franchise record that would almost certainly never be broken. But the 2005 Royals proved up to the challenge, riding a 19-game losing streak to set a new mark with 106 defeats. Pena was out, Buddy Bell was in. Not much changed. The team again reached the century mark in losses in 2006. A once-proud franchise had become the laughingstock of baseball. *Tonight Show* host Jay Leno made the Royals a frequent target, hitting them with quips like, "Kansas City has the only stadium where the good seats are the ones where you don't face the field."

Kansas City improved in 2007, losing a mere 93 games. But the team's fourth consecutive last-place finish ended Buddy Bell's tenure as manager. His replacement, Trey Hillman, led KC out of the cellar with a 75-87 mark in 2008. A 97-loss season followed. Zack Greinke won the AL Cy Young in 2009, but Royals fans had little else to cheer about as another decade passed with no postseason baseball.

THE PROCESS

Greinke becoming just the third Royals pitcher to win a Cy Young Award was not the only significant development for Kansas City baseball during the first decade of the 21st century. Contrary to the impression held by millions of fans, Royals owner David Glass had grown tired of losing. Described by Sam Walton as "whip smart," Glass had been a driving force in Walmart's emergence as the largest retailer in the world. For a man used to winning, the Royals became an embarrassing failure in the career of one of America's most successful businessmen. Though he did not know exactly how to right the ship, the owner decided that something major had to change with his franchise.

In 2006 Glass flew to Atlanta to talk to Braves assistant GM Dayton Moore. Having heard many good things about this man, the owner asked Moore if he could turn his team around. The 39-year-old Braves executive responded that he could—but it would be a slow process. Glass would need to loosen his grip and spend more money. Aside from that, Moore had just one other suggestion: the Royals needed a complete operations makeover.

Glass bought the young executive's pitch. In May 2006 he fired his general manager Allard Baird and hired Moore. The new GM knew that turning around a moribund franchise would not be easy—he labeled his job the greatest challenge in professional sports. He hated to leave Atlanta, where he had a good chance to succeed John Schuerholz, but Moore was excited about the opportunity in KC. "I grew up a Kansas City Royals fan and remember that great tradition," he said. Indeed, as a 19-

year-old college student, Moore had interrupted a road trip home to watch Game 7 of the 1985 World Series from a hilltop outside Royals Stadium.

Backed by Glass's checkbook and a promise of autonomy, Moore moved quickly to improve franchise infrastructure, especially player development. The new GM believed the best way to construct a championship team was to build the best farm system. Kansas City expanded its staff, adding executives and scouts with proven baseball records. Among the most notable hires were Marlins scout Gene Watson and Braves director of minor league operations J.J. Picollo.

The franchise revitalized its international program and built new baseball facilities in Latin America. The Royals invested more money in finding amateur talent and added a minor league team to their farm system. Player salaries meanwhile increased.

Moore furthermore worked to instill a new winning attitude throughout the organization. Minor leaguers had to take a Royals history class to learn about George Brett, Frank White, Dennis Leonard, and the team's past glory seasons. Current players gained a new respect for their franchise and the name on their jerseys.

To complete the franchise makeover, Kansas City renovated its ballpark. Glass invested $25 million, while taxpayers put up $225 million for a stadium upgrade that included a state-of-the-art high-definition crown video board, new suites and club seating, expanded concessions, a new sports bar restaurant, a Hall of Fame building, an activity area for kids, and a 360-degree concourse. The new Kauffman Stadium opened in April 2009. While retaining the picturesque charm of the original design, the upgrade gave the Royals a modern facility for the 21st century.

Results on the field, however, came slowly. To many fans, it seemed that little had changed under Moore's direction. The team lost 93 games during his first full season. Moore replaced Buddy Bell with Trey Hillman to spur a resurgence. Instead, the losing continued. And it would continue under Hillman's successor, Ned Yost. Yost's second full season, 2012, marked the fourth consecutive 90-loss campaign for the Royals.

Grumbling increased about the failures of the new administration. Patience wore thin. Moore maintained that building a winning team took time, and asked people to trust "The Process." Fans and commentators remained skeptical. Some owners would have fired Moore, but Glass still believed in his young GM: "I've learned that the best thing I can do is let him [Moore] do it his way and support him."

Glass would be rewarded for this faith. Even as the losses piled up, the Royals were changing from within. Draft picks started to blossom in the minors. The team found talented young players through its international program. Moore converted the soon-to-be-departing Greinke into two of the Brewers most promising young players. Scouts for other teams envied the growing arsenal in the Royals farm system.

Then, in a move that showed just how much things had changed, Kansas City traded its top hitting prospect Wil Myers for Tampa Bay ace James Shields in December 2012. Rather than shipping off a high-priced top-of-the-rotation pitcher, the Royals were acquiring one. The team was spending money to field a contender. Kansas City's payroll hit $81.7 million in 2013, nearly quadruple the $22.3 million the team spent in 2000.

But spending money does not guarantee success. Neither does taking a team in a new direction. After Kansas City lost 90 games in 2012, the question remained: *Are the Royals heading in the right direction?*

In 2013 Kansas City finished 86-76, the team's best record in nearly a quarter century.

Chapter 4

February–April: A New Hope

Winter storms blasted Kansas City the first week of February 2014, burying Jackson County under nearly a foot of snow. The accumulations wreaked havoc on travel throughout the metro area and surrounding regions. By the middle of the month weather conditions improved, with temperatures climbing to the 40s and 50s. More good news for Kansas Citians was soon to arrive from a thousand miles away. In Surprise, Arizona, Alex Gordon, Billy Butler, James Shields and the rest of the Royals reported for spring training. Expectations for the new season were lofty—perhaps higher than for any upcoming Kansas City campaign since George Brett retired. The team had finished the previous season strong with a 47-34 mark in the second half. After June, only the Los Angeles Dodgers had a better regular season record.

With three Gold Glove winners and two other nominees, Kansas City deployed an elite defense. The team's formidable bullpen also ranked as one of the league's best. James Shields gave the Royals a true top-of-the-rotation ace and Jeremy Guthrie had emerged as a 15-game winner. And the KC lineup featured several guys who could handle the bat. The best Royal slash line (batting average/on base percentage/slugging average) came from Eric Hosmer: .302/.353/.448. Alex Gordon, Salvador

Perez, and Billy Butler also delivered the offensive goods in 2013.

In addition, Dayton Moore had bolstered his team with key offseason acquisitions. A December trade with Milwaukee landed outfielder Nori Aoki, a .286 hitter with 20 stolen bases the previous year. Moore also signed Omar Infante, a slick-fielding second baseman who batted .318 in 2013. Arriving from the farm, flamethrower Yordano Ventura prepared to break into the Royals starting rotation.

Kansas City finished the 2014 Cactus League schedule with 12 wins, 16 losses, and 2 ties. If taken at face value, this mediocre record could have dampened much of the optimism shining on the team. But why would anyone take that record at face value? They were spring training games. Glorified practices. An opportunity to try out new players, many of whom would not even make the big league roster. The games did not count.

A deeper examination of the Cactus League results revealed that the rumors of Kansas City's contender status were well founded. Starters Shields, Ventura, and Jason Vargas shined in their mound opportunities. And Royals hitters tore the cover off the ball, especially third baseman Mike Moustakas who batted over .400 in the desert. Newcomers Aoki and Infante, batting first and second, also hit well, suggesting the top of Yost's lineup would provide plenty of RBI opportunities for the sluggers that followed.

On the downside, one of KC's most effective bullpen weapons, Luke Hochevar, suffered a partially-torn ulnar collateral ligament during spring training. He would undergo Tommy John surgery and miss the entire '14 campaign. Losing a reliever who delivered a 1.92 ERA the previous season would hurt, but hopes remained high for the team. Even after his injury, Hochevar himself noted as much. "The way the team's shaping up, we're going to win," he said. "That's not a doubt."

Baseball analysts still harbored questions about the Royals. Aside from Shields, how would the rest of the rotation hold up?

A valid concern given the loss of innings-eating starter Ervin Santana and his 3.24 ERA to free agency. And could the offense live up to its potential and score enough runs? Kansas City had ranked 11th out of 15 American League clubs in runs scored in 2013. These potential flaws, as well as the team's long playoff drought, convinced oddsmakers that they were still longshots. The sportsbook Bovada set Kansas City's odds of winning the 2014 World Series at 33 to 1. Nonetheless, as Opening Day approached, optimism abounded among the Royals faithful.

OUT OF THE GATE

"Opening Day is always a good day.... Everyone's got hopes up." – Buck O'Neil

Kansas City opened the 2014 season on March 31st at Detroit, home of the defending AL Central champions. Not an easy assignment. Kansas City took an early lead in the Opening Day contest, but Detroit clawed back to tie the game at three heading into the ninth. In the bottom of the inning, Wade Davis, a starter for the Royals in 2013, yielded a walk and a single. Yost brought in Greg Holland, his star closer who had racked up 47 saves the previous season. Tigers shortstop Alex Gonzalez greeted Holland with a single to drive in the winning run. The Royals had played hard, but fell just short against one of the AL's top teams. That was no consolation to Holland. "We're not here to fight and compete," he said. "We're here to win."

Kansas City starter Jason Vargas turned in a stellar effort in the second game of the season, surrendering only one run in seven innings. But Tigers ace Max Scherzer topped him, blanking the Royals through eight. KC tied it 1-1 in the ninth against Detroit reliever Joe Nathan. In the bottom of the tenth, Tigers second baseman Ian Kinsler singled in the winning run to drop the Royals to 0-2. The vaunted KC bullpen had failed twice in a row—not an auspicious start to the season.

The Royals returned to Kauffman Stadium for the team's home opener against Chicago on April 4th. Despite yielding four runs in 5.2 innings, Jeremy Guthrie picked up the win. Kansas City prevailed again the next day, before dropping the series finale against the White Sox. Tampa Bay arrived for a three-game set. In the opening contest, a fastball crashed into Omar Infante's face. Spitting blood, he had to be removed from the game. Though suffering a sprained jaw and a laceration that needed stitches, the Kansas City second baseman would miss only two games.

The teams split the first two contests. In the rubber game against Tampa Bay, Alex Gordon hit the Royals' first home run of the season—a towering three-run shot to right propel KC to a 7-3 victory. Gordon finished with four RBI, equaling his career high for a single game. It was an encouraging sign for a team that was struggling to score runs.

Born in Lincoln, Nebraska, just a three-hour drive from Kauffman Stadium, **Alex Gordon** developed into one of the finest prep ballplayers in the state's history. A four-year starter at Lincoln Southeast, Gordon batted over .500 his final two seasons and led the state in home runs as a junior. His torrid hitting garnered numerous awards and national attention. Despite interest from Tennessee and Baylor, Gordon followed in the footsteps of his father Mike by playing college ball for the University of Nebraska.

As the Cornhuskers' third baseman, Gordon emerged as one of the best college hitters in the country. He captured back-to-back Big 12 Player of the Year honors and led Nebraska to a conference title and an appearance in the 2005 College World Series. Along with teammate Joba Chamberlain, Gordon attracted scores of big league scouts to Husker games. The Royals selected Gordon with the second overall pick of the 2005 draft. Visions of the second coming of George Brett swept Royals Nation.

Continuing his prolific hitting, Gordon made it to The Show after just a year and a half in the minors. However, carrying the expectations of equaling the best player in franchise history did not help the young third baseman. Gordon batted just .247 his rookie year. He improved to .260 his second year, but lost most of the 2009 season to injury. The errors, meanwhile, piled up at third base. After three seasons, it seemed that a shaky glove was Gordon's only similarity with a young George Brett.

The low point came in 2010, when an early-season slump dropped Gordon's average below .200. In May the team demoted him to AAA Omaha. More ominously, management had its eye on another promising young player to take over third base. Dayton Moore told Gordon he wanted him to try to learn to play the outfield. In other words, unless Gordon could learn a position he had not played since high school, his days as a Royal might be numbered. Many observers started shoveling dirt on the grave of the former Cornhusker's big league career. *USA Today*'s Bob Nightengale wrote, "The Kansas City Royals, who admittedly blew it by taking Alex Gordon with the No. 2 pick in the 2005 draft instead of several All-Stars, are hoping to now salvage their choice by moving Gordon to left field."

Though it took some time and a few missteps along the way, Gordon made progress. He spent up to 90 minutes *before* practice each day absorbing lessons from field instructor Rusty Kuntz on how to play outfield. Drawing on his experience as a wide receiver in high school, Gordon applied Kuntz's wisdom to learn the art of taking proper angles when tracking fly balls. Seeking every opportunity to improve, he patrolled the outfield during the team's batting practices. Laboring tirelessly, the young ballplayer displayed an ethic learned from his mother Leslie, who ran an antique store in addition to working long night shift hours as a nurse. As Danny Duffy later observed about Gordon, "He's the hardest worker I've ever met in my life. There's not a close second."

When Kansas City promoted Gordon back to the big league club after six weeks, he had developed into a decent fielder. Decent soon became outstanding as Kansas City's new left fielder gained a reputation for an accurate cannon arm. A season later, Gordon led the majors in outfield assists with 20. The shift to a new position also helped other aspects of his game. As he noted, "I don't think I was the best third baseman, so I think in every game, my focus wasn't on hitting, and more on, 'How am I going to screw up at third base today?'"

This improved mental focus complimented Gordon's rigorous training and dietary regimen. He worked out each day, building his core with hours of cardio and stretching. All the while he ate healthy foods such as grilled chicken, whole wheat pasta, and vegetables. Even in college, the fitness-minded Gordon had avoided junk food.

To improve at the plate Gordon worked with hitting coach Kevin Seitzer, who put him through an intense series of drills and exercises. Remarkable results followed. In 2011 the left fielder topped .300 for the first time as a big leaguer. His power numbers increased as well, with 123 doubles and 57 homers in the three years of 2011-2013. As for fielding, Gordon not only learned his position, he became the best in the business— winning three straight Gold Gloves in that span. Labeled a draft-bust just four years earlier, by April 2014 Gordon represented a potential MVP candidate.

A HARBINGER?

After taking two of three from Tampa Bay, the Royals packed their bags for a six-game road trip. Their first stop was Target Field in Minneapolis, where the Twins pounded KC starter Bruce Chen for six runs in 3.2 innings. Minnesota followed with two more wins to sweep the series. The Royals dropped to 0-5 in road games. Not the stuff of pennant contenders.

Flying south to Houston, the team rebounded to sweep three from the Astros, before returning home for a three-game set with the Twins. After taking the first two games against Minnesota, the Royals had built a five-game winning streak to improve to 9-7 on the year. Even better, the team moved into a tie with the Tigers for first place in the division.

Was this mid-April surge a harbinger of bigger things to come for the Boys in Blue? If the answer to that question were to be a yes, more of the team's young sluggers would need to start raking. In the second game at Houston, Mike Moustakas hammered a solo blast in the eleventh to put the Royals ahead for good. The timely homer raised hopes that the man at third base might soon be finding his stroke.

When Dayton Moore asked Gordon to shift positions in 2010, **Mike Moustakas** was a major reason why. At Chatsworth High School in the Los Angeles metropolitan area, "Moose," as his teammates called him, set the California single-season and career record for home runs. He also starred on USA Baseball's Junior National team in 2006. The following summer, Baseball America named him the High School Player of the Year. In the June 2007 draft, Kansas City selected Moose as the second overall pick—same as Gordon two years earlier. One benefit of all those losing seasons was that KC consistently landed a good position in the draft.

Passing on the opportunity to play college ball at USC, Moustakas signed with the Royals in a deal that included a $4 million bonus. The nephew of longtime big league hitting coach Tom Robson, Moose brought tape-measure power and a competitive spirit to his new employers. He had inherited a strong will to win from his father Mike, a retired attorney and former UCLA football player. As Moustakas said about his dad, "I hate losing and that's what he ingrained in me." Moose also credits his father for advice that helped keep him motivated. "If you're not out working hard," Mike Sr. told his son, "someone's working harder."

After showing some promise in Class A ball, Moustakas erupted for 36 home runs (tied for tops in the minors) and 124 RBI for AA Northwest Arkansas and AAA Omaha in 2010. Kansas City called him up in June 2011, when he was just 22 years old. Moose posted respectable numbers his rookie season, batting .263 in 89 games. He followed with an impressive 20 home runs and 73 RBI in 2012. Though his average and power numbers dipped (.233/.287/.364) in 2013, the organization remained committed to Moustakas as its everyday third baseman. The infielder's willingness to learn reinforced the team's confidence in the young man. After working with Moose at a Royals training camp, George Brett commented, "He's always open to suggestion, anything to get better, and those are the types of guys that get better."

A torrid hitting run at spring training boosted club expectations that Moustakas was heading for a big year in 2014. April, however, proved to be prime Moose-hunting season for AL pitchers, who gunned him down night after night. The eleventh-inning home run in Houston stirred optimism that the young slugger was poised for a breakout. For Moustakas, unfortunately, the worst was yet to come.

TREADING WATER

The Royals' five-game winning streak ended with an 8-3 drubbing in the series finale against Minnesota on April 20th. The team traveled to Cleveland, where they dropped three of four to the Tribe. Kansas City's road trip continued in Baltimore, where eight shutout innings by Yordano Ventura yielded a victory in the first contest. The following night at Camden Yards, Kansas City and Baltimore completed nine innings knotted at two. In the tenth, Royals reliever Danny Duffy loaded the bases with nobody out. Ned Yost brought in Louis Coleman, who surrendered an RBI single. The loss was the Royals' fifth in their last seven games, dropping the team below .500. After nearly a month of baseball Kansas City was 11-12, three games off the division lead. The momentum of the second half of 2013 had fizzled in the spring chill of another mediocre April.

The season, of course, was still early. And Royals fans had plenty of reasons to remain hopeful that their boys would heat up with the coming warmer temperatures—just as earlier editions of the team had done in the 1970s and 1980s. With Billy Butler mired in a .209 slump thus far, the 2014 squad had yet to benefit from one of its most reliable hitters. Lofty RBI totals from the longest-tenured Royal had been one of the few consistent positives to come out of the Trey Hillman era. If Butler could again deliver run-scoring hits as he had in the past, the Boys in Blue would enjoy a much brighter summer.

After emerging as one of Florida's best prep hitters at Wolfson High in Jacksonville, **Billy Butler** signed a letter of intent in 2003 to play for the University of Florida. Gator coaches eagerly awaited the thunder that Butler had brought to Wolfson and the USA Junior National team. But the teen slugger had another suitor in Kansas City, which selected Butler in the first round of the 2004 draft. With a $1.45 million bonus on the table to play professional ball, the young man's post high school plans quickly changed.

Butler destroyed Rookie League pitching en route to a .373 batting average and 1.084 OPS (on-base percentage plus slugging), numbers that ranked him as the top Royals prospect at the end of 2004. Butler continued to knock the cover off the ball as he climbed the KC farm system ladder. In the summer of 2006, he hit a two-run homer to lead Team USA to victory in the Futures Game. His contributions earned him the MVP award for the contest, which also featured two hits from fellow Royals prospect Alex Gordon.

That same year, Butler won the Texas League batting title for the Wichita Wranglers. Though a third baseman in high school, he moved to the outfield for Wichita. After he continued to slug at AAA Omaha, Kansas City called Butler to the majors in May 2007. The rookie posted an impressive slash line (.292/.347/.447) in 92 games for KC. Over the first two months of the 2008 season, however, Butler's average dipped and his power dissipated. With the team mired in a losing streak, management sent him down to AAA to work on his stroke. Wondering if he was being made the scapegoat for the team's woes, Butler expressed his disappointment. "I'd like for them to show confidence in me to get back out of it in the big leagues," he said, "but that's just not the way it works out."

After hitting .337 during his month with Omaha, Butler returned to the majors for good in June 2008. Playing first base and DH, Butler became his team's most consistent run producer over the next five seasons. From 2009 to 2013 he topped .300 three times, while never batting below .289. Butler also drove in at least 90 runs three times in that span, topping out at 107 in 2012 when he was named to the AL All-Star team. Despite playing half his games at spacious Kauffman Stadium, Butler delivered impressive power numbers too, averaging 20 home runs a season over those five years.

One thing Butler, nicknamed "Country Breakfast," did not bring to the table was speed. Heading into 2014, his career stolen base total lingered at a meager five. And he had twice led the league in grounding into double plays. No problem—the Royals had plenty of other guys who could run. Butler was the man who would drive them in. To contend in 2014, the Royals needed Country Breakfast to serve up plenty more heaping helpings of RBI goodness.

Kansas City rebounded from its walk-off defeat at Camden Yards to take the final game of the Baltimore series. Throwing seven strong innings, James Shields picked up his third victory. The Royals returned home to open a three-game set with the Blue Jays. Kansas City prevailed in the first two contests to push its record over .500 again. Played on the last day of April, the second victory over Toronto provided several encouraging signs for KC. Shortstop Alcides Escobar drilled a two-run double; Greg Holland picked up his seventh save; and first baseman Eric Hosmer drove in two runs and smashed two doubles to raise his batting average above .300.

The number-three hitter in the lineup, **Eric Hosmer**—like Gordon, Moustakas, and Butler—had emerged as a fan-favorite and a key component in the Royals' resurgence. Hosmer had displayed an extraordinary talent for baseball as a youth in Cooper City, Florida. His mother Ileana, a nurse who had fled Fidel Castro's Cuba, and his father Mike, a fireman, continually encouraged young Eric's baseball development. Ileana helped her son with his homework and taped his games for him to study, while Mike threw batting practice even after working 48-hour shifts. Hosmer's parents crisscrossed the state driving to baseball tournaments and hired a professional hitting instructor to further their son's progress.

For Hosmer's prep career, his parents enrolled him in American Heritage School, a private institution known for its top-notch baseball program. Hosmer by this time worked out nearly seven hours a day, lifting weights to develop power-hitting muscles. He studied game tape with his older brother Mike Jr. to improve his swing. Eric's batting and fielding exploits in high school attracted droves of professional scouts and college recruiters. Arizona State, one of the top baseball programs in the nation, offered him a scholarship.

Kansas City selected the highly-touted Hosmer with their first pick of the 2008 draft. Represented by agent Scott Boras, Hosmer received a $6 million signing bonus from the Royals—the largest in team history. As with Moustakas a year earlier, negotiations for the contract dragged on, with an agreement being reached only minutes before the signing deadline.

Hosmer struggled with injury during his first full season in the minors, batting just .241 for the year. After laser eye surgery corrected astigmatism problems, his sizzling bat earned him a promotion to AA Northwest Arkansas in 2010. Along with Moose, Hosmer headed a group of potential stars that elevated the Royals farm system to the top of the rankings heading into the 2011 season. Not since Bo Jackson had a Royals prospect elicited such excitement. After Hosmer pounded the ball at a .439 clip during his first month with AAA Omaha, Kansas City promoted him to the bigs on May 5th. Calling the achievement a family effort, the young ballplayer phoned home and said, "We made it."

After reaching The Show, the talented prospect did not disappoint. Taking over first base for the Royals, he batted .293 with 19 homers and 78 RBI—numbers that earned him third place in Rookie of the Year voting. Unfortunately, the dreaded sophomore slump set in the next year. His average dropped to .232, and he hit five fewer home runs.

Hosmer's decline at the plate likely contributed to Yost's decision to fire hitting coach Kevin Seitzer in October 2012. When the team's offensive production lagged at the start of the following season, the Royals convinced George Brett to sign on as hitting coach. During his eight weeks in the position, the best player in franchise history improved Hosmer's technique and inspired a much-needed boost in confidence.

The young first baseman bounced back in a big way his third season. He batted .302 in 2013, with 17 home runs and 79 RBI. Meanwhile, his fielding excellence at first base earned him a Gold Glove Award. With the potential for even bigger numbers in 2014, Eric Hosmer was a major reason why many within the organization predicted the Royals were about to contend for a postseason spot.

With one month in the books, Kansas City trailed the division-leading Tigers by just a game and a half. Sitting at 14-12, things could have gone better and they could have gone worse. After four weeks of baseball, it seemed as if the Royals were at least treading water—keeping their heads above the waves. But such results were not good enough. Not for a team that hoped to keep playing in October.

Chapter 5

May: Mediocrity

After dropping a 7-3 decision to the Blue Jays on May 1st, the Royals prepared for their biggest series of the year thus far. Arriving the next day for three games at The K were the division-leading Detroit Tigers. Former pro wrestling champ "Nature Boy" Ric Flair used to taunt his challengers by proclaiming, "To be the man, you have to beat the man." For Kansas City to be *the man* in the AL Central, they would have to beat the Tigers—winners of three consecutive division titles.

The Royals sent their ace James Shields to the mound for the first game. The Tigers body-slammed him for seven earned runs, while strutting to an 8-2 victory. A night later, Detroit chopped down the home team with nine more runs. And in the series finale the Tigers again scored nine, inflicting more pain than a figure-four leglock. Over the three games, Detroit outscored Kansas City 26 to 8 to drop a humiliating 1-2-3 pin on their outmatched challengers.

The next day, the flagging Royals traveled to San Diego to start a week-long road trip. In the opener, the Padres prevailed in 12 innings to extend Kansas City's losing streak to five. The team dropped into fourth place, just a game and a half above the cellar-dwelling Indians. To make matters worse, persisting back pain sent southpaw starter Bruce Chen to the disabled list. The wheels had not yet come off the KC cart, but the squeaking grew louder.

Game 2 in San Diego again went to extra innings. But this time the Royals emerged victorious after Gordon and Butler delivered RBI hits in the 11th. Earlier in the contest, Kansas City had tied the score with a home run from catcher Salvador Perez. The Royals backstop had caught all 23 innings of the two games in San Diego—a lot of crouching in a short amount of time. Not a problem for the reigning AL Gold Glove winner; Perez would have been out there if each of the games had gone 30 innings.

Growing up in Valencia, Venezuela, **Salvador Perez** started playing ball not long out of the cradle. His mother Yilda Diaz pitched him bottle caps and corn kernels, which he hit with a broomstick. She later took her boy to a baseball school, where he gained recognition for his diamond skills by age six. A talented cook who supported her family by selling lasagna, flan, and cakes, Yilda handled paperwork, rounded up equipment, and attended meetings for her son's youth games. Reflecting on these early years, Perez remained grateful for Yilda's support. "She is not just my mother, she is my friend and my helper," he said. "And don't forget—my grandmother is the very same thing."

Perez became a catcher at age eight, because that position had the shortest line of boys trying out. As a teenager, Salvador's prowess behind the plate attracted the attention of big league scouts. Now a contender for Latin talent, Kansas City signed Perez for $65,000 in September 2006 when he was 16— the age that Latin players become eligible to sign professional baseball contracts. A year later he moved to the United States to play for KC's Rookie-class team in Surprise, Arizona.

Perez advanced rapidly through the Royals farm system. At spring training in 2011, the young catcher impressed Yost and the coaches with his accuracy and quick throws to second base. Royals senior pitching advisor Bill Fischer praised Perez as "the Venezuelan Johnny Bench." Kansas City called him up to the majors in August. He joined Hosmer and Moustakas as Omaha players who became regulars in the KC lineup that year. Over the final seven weeks of the season, Perez tore through big league pitching with a .331/.361/.473 slash line. Kansas City's catcher of the future had arrived.

Perez, however, suffered a setback the following spring training when he tore the meniscus in his left knee while warming up a pitcher. The subsequent knee surgery sidelined him for the first three months of the 2012 season. Perez returned in late June and caught 74 games for the Royals. He batted .301 with 11 home runs and 39 RBI during his half-season.

Logging his first full big league campaign in 2013, Perez emerged as an offensive force in Yost's lineup, batting .292 and driving in 79. Along the way he made the AL All-Star team and won a Gold Glove for his ability to block pitches and gun down runners. An impressive turnaround for a player who by his own admission had little interest in learning defensive fundamentals as a youth in Venezuela.

In addition to Perez's contributions on the field, his fun-loving personality helped keep the Royals clubhouse laid-back and relaxed. He loved to shoot humorous videos of teammates on his iPhone, with Lorenzo Cain as favorite target, and post the clips on Instagram. One time before a game, Alcides Escobar sprayed Perez's jersey with women's perfume. After getting four hits that day, the catcher has worn 212 VIP or Victoria's Secret perfume for every game since. Four out of five home plate umpires agree: Salvador Perez is the best-smelling catcher in the league.

REBOUND

Kansas City won the rubber game in San Diego behind seven shutout innings from Shields. The team then traveled north for a four-game set against Seattle. After Mariner starter Hisashi Iwakuma silenced Royal bats in the opener, Jason Vargas tossed seven scoreless innings to take the second game. The teams split the next two contests to finish the series 2-2.

Returning home, Kansas City swept two games from Colorado. The short series featured more stellar pitching from Shields and Vargas. The two starters had thus far accounted for nine of KC's 20 wins. On the offensive side, Lorenzo Cain and Alcides Escobar combined for five hits in 12 at-bats, with two walks, two runs scored, and four RBI against the Rockies. With his team having won six of its last eight, Ned Yost had to feel good about this production from the former Brewers anchoring the lower part of his lineup.

Like Perez, **Alcides Escobar** started playing baseball as a young boy in Venezuela. Growing up, he idolized countryman Omar Vizquel, winner of nine straight Gold Gloves from 1993-2001. Developing fielding skills that would have made his hero proud, the teenage Escobar attracted interest from major league scouts. Milwaukee signed him at age 16 for $35,000 in 2003.

Rising through the Brewers farm system, Escobar displayed considerable offensive talents to compliment his defensive wizardry at shortstop. In six minor league seasons, the young Venezuelan batted .293 and stole 176 bases, including 42 for AAA Nashville in 2009. When the Brewers called him up to the bigs later that year, he battled .304 in 38 games.

In 2010 Escobar's numbers dipped to .235/.288/.326. His defensive skills nonetheless made him the everyday shortstop for Milwaukee. The organization at this time assessed the veteran talent it had assembled. With several stars like Prince Fielder who would not be around much longer, the club decided to make a play to win now. His goal set, Brewers general manager Doug Melvin eyed Royals Cy Young-winner Zack Greinke as an ace starter who could put his team over the top.

Meanwhile in Kansas City, Greinke had expressed his discontentment at playing for a losing team. With a high-priced, disgruntled pitcher he was certain to lose to free agency in two seasons, Dayton Moore was willing to make a deal with Melvin.

In December 2010, the Royals sent Greinke and shortstop Yuniesky Betancourt to Milwaukee in exchange for Escobar, two talented young pitchers, and a promising centerfielder.

Though he paid a hefty price, Melvin got what he wanted in the deal. Continuing his run as one of the premier starters in the game, Greinke went 16-6 for Milwaukee in 2011. The Crew won their division and reached the league championship series for the first time in nearly three decades.

As for Kansas City, the deal worked out there as well. Escobar gave the Royals one of the top fielding shortstops in the league. He also became an offensive threat, batting .293 with 35 stolen bases in 2012. Though his stats dipped the following year, Escobar's strong start (.285 through mid-May) suggested the shortstop was headed for a bounce back season in 2014.

The benefits of the Greinke trade did not end with Escobar. Also arriving from Milwaukee in December 2010 was **Lorenzo Cain**, the promising centerfielder included in the deal. Unlike Escobar, Cain got a late start with baseball, not playing the game until tenth grade. Cain's father died when he was four, so his mother Patricia worked two jobs to support her two sons. Young Lorenzo chose not to add sports to her burdens. Only when he got cut from the basketball team in high school did he seriously consider checking out the diamond.

The gangly teen seemed the unlikeliest of future baseball stars when he showed up at tryouts in jeans and tennis shoes. Cain brought to the field no glove and no baseball experience—other than hitting tennis balls in backyard games. Fortunately, the baseball team at Madison County High, a small school in the Florida panhandle, lacked players. Needing warm bodies just to field a team, Coach Barney Myers gave the skinny kid a shot.

Cain struggled with nearly every aspect of the game. He threw off the wrong foot; he held the bat with crossed wrists; he did not understand the rules. Not surprisingly, he rode the bench his first season of prep ball. But Cain liked being on the team—being a part of something. So he started working out like a maniac. He logged countless hours with the pitching machine and fielded innumerable fly balls hit to him by Myers *after* practice. This hard work, combined with rare natural talent, allowed a ballplayer to emerge.

After Cain turned in a strong senior season at Madison County High, Milwaukee drafted him in the 17th round of the 2004 draft. Several years behind the other players in development, Cain struggled at times in the minors. Wrestling with homesickness and disappointment at his failures, he told his mother he wanted to quit. She talked him into sticking with the game. It did not take long for Cain's talent and work ethic to vault him up the Brewers farm system.

In July 2010 Milwaukee promoted Cain to The Show. He batted .306 and stole seven bases in 43 games for the Crew. Combining this offensive potential with his impressive range, it seemed that the Brewers centerfielder of the future had arrived. Until Doug Melvin called Cain's agent Joshua Kusnick in December 2010 with news of the trade.

Cain spent most of his first season with the Royals playing for AAA Omaha. Though ready to make the next step as an everyday major leaguer in 2012, injuries limited him to just 61 games for KC that season. Bouncing back, Cain emerged from 2013 spring training as the Royals regular centerfielder. But he again battled injuries during the season and hit just .251 in 115 games. Nonetheless, the exceptional speed and range he displayed in spacious Kauffman Stadium fueled expectations for bigger and better things. His .319 average through six weeks of the 2014 campaign suggested that a healthy Cain would go a long way in furthering a Royals playoff run.

HEADING NOWHERE

After sweeping Colorado, the Royals opened a four-game series against Baltimore at The K. Scoring just one run over eighteen innings, Kansas City dropped the first two games. Royal bats remained cold in the third game, but fortunately Danny Duffy and the bullpen shut out the O's to prevail 1-0. The KC offense finally came alive the next night, led by a combined seven hits from Gordon and Butler, to split the series 2-2.

After dropping two of three to the White Sox at Kauffman, the Royals prepared to fly west to take on the Los Angeles Angels. But their third baseman would not be making this trip. Mired in a prolonged slump that plunged his batting average to .152, Mike Moustakas was heading to AAA Omaha. He thus joined Alex Gordon and Billy Butler as promising stars demoted to the minors mid-season. Praising his player's heart and passion, Moore insisted that this was just a "reset" and that Moustakas remained an important part of the team. "He'll go down there and experience success," the GM said, "and we look forward to his contributions when he returns."

The Moose-less Royals lost two out of three to the Angels. Eric Hosmer's four hits and a rally-igniting double from third baseman Danny Valencia were the highlights of Kansas City's lone win at Angel Stadium.

The team flew home for a three-game set against the Astros. Having dropped back-to-back series, Kansas City received some much-needed good news with the return of Infante. The Royals had been without their regular second baseman for three weeks due to a lower back injury.

At 32, **Omar Infante** was the oldest starting position player in the Royals 2014 lineup. Detroit had signed the Venezuelan infielder in 1999 when he was 17 years old. Just as it seemed his baseball dreams were coming true, nightmarish tragedies followed. His brother Asdrubal, a pitcher in the Tigers system, was shot and killed later that year. Infante's family then started receiving death threats. Omar began carrying a gun and moved his family to a different town in Venezuela. Two years later, his father died from a heart attack.

Remaining determined, Infante did not let these blows stop him. "My brother and my dad are my motivation to keep working hard and do my best," he said. "It was their dream to see me make it; I want to keep that dream alive." His teammate Mike Rivera echoed that sentiment: "So much has happened to him at a young age, but I think all of it will help to make him even stronger." Detroit GM Randy Smith similarly retained his faith in Infante. Quoting Tigers coach Luis Pujols, Smith said, "Omar is a good player, but an even better man."

With stellar glove work, Infante advanced quickly in the Tigers farm system. He reached the AA level by age 19, earning Best Defensive Shortstop distinction in the Eastern League. His debut in the majors came in 2002 with a September call-up. After splitting the following season between Detroit and Triple-A Toledo, Infante took over as the Tigers everyday shortstop in 2004. His batting, long considered a weakness, improved to .264/.317/.449.

After Infante slumped in 2005, Detroit relegated him to part-time status the following two seasons. The Tigers then shipped him to Atlanta, where he regained his hitting stroke. In 2010 Infante batted .321 and earned a spot on the NL All-Star team. Following the season Atlanta traded him to the Marlins for slugging second baseman Dan Uggla. A year and a half later, Detroit reacquired Infante in a trade.

As a free agent after the 2013 season, Infante appeared on Dayton Moore's radar. The GM needed a second baseman. Once manned by Frank White, the best in the business, this position had been a revolving-door for the Royals throughout Moore's tenure. He signed Infante to a four-year $30.25 million contract. In addition to bringing stability to the middle infield, Moore hoped his veteran acquisition could mentor fellow Venezuelan Alcides Escobar.

The 2014 season brought unexpected challenges for Infante. A sore elbow hampered his throwing. The aforementioned encounter with an early-season fastball cut open his jaw. And he spent most of May on the disabled list with a back ailment. In addition, a sore shoulder would vex Infante all season, eventually requiring the drug Toradol to manage the pain.

Infante hit a double and helped turn two double plays in his first game back from the DL. That was about the only good news for the Royals, who got drubbed 9-2 by the Astros. Making matters worse, KC would lose Yordano Ventura for at least one start due to valgus extension overload (aka pitcher's elbow). Houston then took the next two games from the Royals. And so the lowly, last-place Astros, boasting the worst record in the American League, swept Kansas City at Kauffman Stadium.

Licking their wounds, the Royals flew to Canada for a four-game series against Toronto. Seeking to wake up an offense that ranked last in the AL in runs scored and slugging percentage, the team replaced hitting coach Pedro Grifol with third base coach and former Cubs skipper Dale Sveum. Mike Jirschele took over coaching duties at third. The team responded with 14 hits, including three RBI from Infante, in an extra-inning victory the first game north of the border. Vargas's strong pitching netted a win in the second contest, but the Blue Jays roughed up Aaron Brooks in his first career start to take Game 3. For the series finale on June 1st, Moustakas rejoined the team. Unfortunately, Toronto ace Mark Buehrle silenced Royal bats to split the series.

Kansas City had dropped six of its last eight games to fall to 26-30. Following their shutout loss to close out the Toronto series, the team descended to the bottom of the AL Central. When David Glass hired Dayton Moore in May 2006, the team was in last place. When Moore hired Ned Yost in May 2010, the team was again in last place. Now, eight years into Moore's term and four years into Yost's, the Royals had returned to the cellar. Moore, Yost, and the coaching staff insisted that things had changed. But two months into this once-promising season, the Royals again seemed to be heading nowhere. As fan frustrations increased, attendance waned. Kansas City's pro soccer team, Sporting KC, outdrew the Royals when the two teams hosted home games the same evening in late May. Articles and commentaries further reflected the growing disappointment in the baseball team's declining fortunes. "There is still plenty of season left," wrote Connor Moylan for Royals Review after the

Astros series, "but it's hard not to feel like the year is shot and the Royals will miss the postseason yet again." Joe Posnanski, who formerly covered the team for *The Kansas City Star*, declared that of all the American sports teams, the Royals were the hardest to love.

Dark clouds gathered over The K. Kansas City's hitting coach had already lost his job. Were more changes higher up soon to follow?

Chapter 6

June: The Streak

On June 2nd, the Royals traveled to St. Louis for the first of four consecutive games against their in-state rivals. The annual interleague contests between Major League Baseball's two Missouri teams had developed into one of the most anticipated regular season series of the year.

As baseball rivalries go, the I-70 version was relatively young. Through the 1970s and first half of the 1980s, there was no Show-Me State rivalry at all. Interleague play did not exist, and the teams never faced each other in the postseason. Then came 1985. The World Series that year could have been a paragon of quality baseball and professional sportsmanship, in which both victor and vanquished parted with mutual respect. But instead, the series turned on an umpire's blown call in Game 6, followed by an embarrassing meltdown and raging tempers in Game 7. Bitterness lingered among the many Cardinal players and fans who would never forget the world championship that was "stolen" from them.

The Cardinals rebounded to capture the NL pennant in 1987, before hitting a dry spell that lasted nearly a decade. After Tony La Russa's arrival in St. Louis in 1996, the Redbirds again became a fixture in the postseason. Kansas City's fortunes, in contrast, had waned by this time. As a result, a different sort of bitterness festered in western Missouri. Like a younger sibling overshadowed by a celebrated older brother, Kansas City faded into obscurity. Outshined by the successes of the red-feathered franchise to the east, KC became Missouri's "other" team that had no part in the national baseball conversation—unless as a punch line.

But the Royals always had one thing over the Cardinals: 1985. No matter how many pennants the Cardinals won or how many 100-loss seasons the Royals endured, nothing could change the outcome of the 1985 World Series. And Kansas Citians did not let their friends on the Mississippi side of the state forget it. Even decades later, fans wearing blue loved to drop the name Dane Iorg when conversing with their red-clad counterparts.

Among the many innovations during Bud Selig's tenure as baseball commissioner was the inauguration of interleague play. Through nearly the entire twentieth century, teams in the National League never faced teams in the American League in the regular season. But in 1997, interleague play became part of the summer schedule. Major League Baseball sought to increase attendance and interest by promoting geography-based rivalries. The Yankees vs. the Mets. The White Sox vs. the Cubs. The A's vs. the Giants. And of course, the Royals vs. the Cardinals.

From 1997 to 2013, the two Missouri teams played three to six games against each other every year. Given that this era featured the nadir of Royals baseball and a Cardinal team that reached the postseason on a near-annual basis, the results were not surprising. Heading into 2014, St. Louis owned a 45-31 record against their in-state rivals.

Past results, however, did not matter much to the two squads preparing to square off at Busch Stadium on June 2, 2014. Yes, Missouri bragging rights were on the line, but the participants on both sides had more immediate concerns. Trailing the division-leading Brewers by four games, the Cardinals hoped for a hot streak to vault them to the top of the NL Central. And the Royals sought to right the ship after a late May slide.

The first chapter of the 2014 I-70 rivalry unfolded as a pitchers' duel, with Danny Duffy and Cardinals starter Shelby Miller matching each other through six scoreless frames. In the top of the seventh, Alex Gordon broke the tie with a 425-foot blast to right. Three more Royal hits followed, including a two-run double from Mike Moustakas. Kansas City added three in the eighth to coast to a 6-0 triumph.

The Cards prepared to deliver some payback in Game 2 after Kolton Wong's grand slam staked the birds to an early 4-0 lead. But Kansas City exploded for six runs in the fifth inning, capped off by Gordon's three-run tater. St. Louis battled back, and the teams entered the ninth tied at seven. Facing Cardinal closer Trevor Rosenthal, Omar Infante doubled and scored the go-ahead run on a hit from Eric Hosmer. Greg Holland retired the home team in order in the bottom of the ninth to pick up his 16th save.

The teams headed west for two more games at Kauffman Stadium. Silenced for eight innings by Cardinal ace Adam Wainwright, the Royal bats awoke for two runs in the ninth to tie the game. The demoralized Cardinals headed into extra innings with the prospect of dropping three straight to their in-state rival. Third baseman Matt Carpenter came to the rescue for St. Louis in the eleventh, drilling his fifth hit of the night to break the tie. Two more Cardinal runs sent the thousands of redbird fans at The K home happy.

Winners of eight straight at Kauffman, the Cardinals looked to split the four-game series behind 2013 postseason hero Michael Wacha. Kansas City countered with its own young mound star, Yordano Ventura. Both pitchers threw well, but the Cards led 2-0 heading to the bottom of the sixth. Alcides Escobar led off the frame with a rally-igniting double. Three more Royal hits followed to put the home team up 3-2. The bullpen preserved the narrow lead, giving KC three out of four against St. Louis.

After their 1985 World Series foe departed, the Royals' 1970s tormenters arrived in town for a four-game set. Yankee rookie Chase Whitley held Kansas City batters in check to claim the first contest 4-2. The Royals rebounded to take the next two from the Bombers. Rain washed out the series finale, disappointing the many fans hoping to see Yankee shortstop Derek Jeter in his final game at The K.

Kansas City swept two games from Cleveland to complete an impressive 5-2 home stand. Traveling to Chicago, the team blasted the White Sox by a combined score of 16-3 in the first two games in the Windy City. These victories gave the Royals a six-game winning streak. In the last five of those contests, the Kansas City starter (Shields, Vargas, Ventura, Guthrie, Duffy) had picked up the victory. It was no secret that pitching coach Dave Eiland directed one of the top bullpens in the league. Now his starters looked to be hitting their stride.

THE ROTATION

James Shields graduated in 2000 from William S. Hart High, a Newhall, California institution known for its strong athletic programs. Indeed, by this time the Santa Clarita Valley school had already given the majors an emerging star in Kevin Millar, 1990s catcher Todd Zeile, and 1980s hurler Bob Walk. As a prep ace, Shields received the nickname "Big Game James" from his Hart High teammates. After a back injury shelved him for most of his senior year, his draft stock fell. Not till the 16th Round of the 2000 draft did Tampa Bay select him. Passing on a scholarship to LSU, Shields signed with the Rays.

Despite a shoulder ailment that required surgery, Shields climbed the Tampa Bay farm system ladder. Debuting in the majors two months into the 2006 season, he won his first four starts. Following a respectable rookie campaign, Shields emerged as a top-of-the-rotation arm for Rays manager Joe Maddon. Big Game James played a key role in the team's Cinderella run to the 2008 World Series. With his victory in Game 2 against the Phillies, Shields became the only Rays pitcher ever to win a World Series game.

Following two subpar seasons, Shields stormed back in 2011, winning 16 games with a 2.82 ERA. He made the AL All-Star team that year and finished third in Cy Young voting. Deploying one of the league's best change-ups, the right-hander turned in another solid campaign in 2012. That offseason, with Shields due to make $9 million, Tampa Bay started listening to trade offers.

In Kansas City, Dayton Moore and his staff reviewed a list of pitchers that could help make their team a winner. The GM liked what he saw in Shields, a clubhouse leader who devoured innings by the bushel. The pitcher had led the league with 11 complete games and four shutouts in 2011. Blessed with a surplus of young hitters, Moore sent his top slugging prospect Wil Myers to Tampa Bay for Shields. KC also swapped pitching prospect Jake Odorizzi for reliever Wade Davis as part of the deal.

Baseball analysts crucified Moore for making this move. Rob Neyer, the National Baseball Editor for SB Nation, tweeted, "This is the worst trade in MLB history unless Wade Davis becomes a good starter, in which case it's only the second worst." How Moore could surrender one of baseball's top hitting prospects for a high-priced pitcher under contract for just two more years baffled experts.

Despite the withering storm of criticism, Moore got the innings-eating ace he wanted. Shields went 13-9 with a 3.15 ERA for Kansas City in 2013, while leading the American League in innings pitched and tying for the lead in games started. As for Myers, he hit .293/.354/.478 for Tampa Bay and won the AL Rookie of the Year. Haters of the trade continued to hate. How Shields performed in 2014 would determine if Moore really did commit a sin worse than swapping Lou Brock for Ernie Broglio, or Nolan Ryan for Jim Fregosi, or Christy Mathewson for Amos Rusie.

After Shields pitched the Royals past New York on June 8th, his record stood at 7-3 with a 3.44 ERA.

Two nights after Shields's successful outing against the Yankees, **Jason Vargas** tossed seven and two-thirds innings in a victory over Cleveland. Like Shields, he was a product of southern California, graduating from Apple Valley High School in the High Desert in 2001. Apple Valley Coach Sean Sers appreciated his competitive nature, later recalling that Vargas "was not scared of anybody or anything." A complimentary ability to remain calm on the mound would become one of the young pitcher's greatest assets moving forward.

Although the Minnesota Twins drafted him in the 43rd round of the 2001 draft, Vargas opted to play college ball at LSU. After his freshman year with the Tigers, the athletic lefty became homesick and transferred to Cypress College in California. The move to junior college resulted in more innings, a lower ERA, and a higher batting average (.374) for Vargas. His peripatetic college career continued at Long Beach State for his junior season. After Vargas helped the Dirtbags reach the NCAA Super Regionals, the Miami Marlins selected him in the second round of the 2004 draft.

Logging only a year of minor league ball, Vargas made his major league debut in July 2005 at the age of 22. After a promising rookie season, he fell victim to a sophomore slump the following year. With his ERA ballooning over 7.00, he found himself back in the minors with AAA Albuquerque. The Marlins traded Vargas to the New York Mets in November 2006. His new employers similarly assigned the lefty to their Triple-A team.

After a torn hip labrum shelved Vargas for the entire 2008 season, the Mets shipped him to Seattle. His first year with the Mariners again saw the southpaw bouncing between AAA and the bigs. Finally in 2010 he landed a spot in Seattle's rotation. He progressed with the Mariners, peaking in 2012 with a 14-11 record and a 3.85 ERA. Despite that successful campaign, Seattle traded him to the Angels in the off-season. After winning nine games for Los Angeles in 2013, Vargas became a free agent.

Vargas had impressed Royals management by twice shutting them down in 2013. His change-up frustrated KC hitters, especially Eric Hosmer who managed only one hit in 13 at-bats against him. Seeking a steady starter to replace the departing Ervin Santana, Royals scouts noted Vargas's poise and composed nature. And as a fly ball pitcher, the reliable southpaw seemed a good fit for spacious Kauffman Stadium.

In November 2013 Kansas City signed Vargas to a four-year $32 million deal. That total marked the second largest signing for a pitcher in franchise history.

Following Vargas in the rotation was rookie **Yordano Ventura**. On June 11th, he allowed just one run over seven innings to complete a two-game sweep over the Indians. Growing up in the resort town of Las Terrenas on the northern Dominican coast, Ventura first displayed his cannon arm as a shortstop. Quitting school at age 14, he mixed concrete and lugged heavy blocks for a construction company. Three years later, Royals scout Pedro Silverio spotted Yordano firing 90-mph fastballs at the ballpark in Las Terrenas. Though the kid was scrawny (just 5'6" and 125 pounds), Silverio convinced field coordinator Victor Baez to give Ventura a tryout at the Royals Academy in Guerra, near the Dominican capital of Santo Domingo. After plunking a dummy batter in the head with his first two pitches, Ventura settled down and impressed the scouts with his whip-like arm. Baez recommended the young hurler to Rene Francisco, the team's vice president for international operations, who signed the 17-year-old in 2008 for $28,000. Though amateur free agents often command larger bonuses, Yordano knew that few other teams would be willing to take a risk on a pitcher his size.

Ventura spent eighteen months at the Royals Academy in Guerra before arriving in the States for rookie-level ball in 2010. Coaches and talent evaluators took notice of the unusual heat generated by this small-framed kid. A fastball in the high-90s earned him comparisons with his childhood hero Pedro

Martinez. Soon Ventura had a new nickname: "Lil' Pedro." Averaging a strikeout per inning, the young fireballer reached Double-A ball by the end of 2012.

Heading into 2013, all the major baseball publications ranked Ventura as a top prospect. After piling up the strikeouts in Omaha, he debuted in the majors on September 17th. Though his stock rose, some criticized his durability, command, and lack of a quality off-speed pitch. Ventura continued to develop, adding a beguiling change-up to compliment his blazing fastball and power curve.

After Ventura excelled at spring training in 2014, Ned Yost added the 22-year-old to his starting rotation. With heat that reached triple-digits, the phenom's talent was undeniable. But questions remained. Specifically, could a body barely six feet tall and 180 pounds hold up through an entire season? And how exactly could someone that size throw so fast? Scientists sought to find an answer. Medical and mechanical engineering expert Glenn Fleisig explained that Ventura's velocity was the product of the near-perfect timing of the different motions of the pitcher's body parts. Complimenting this synchronicity was the extraordinary functional strength generated by the muscles, tendons, and ligaments that Ventura had honed from years of throwing and swimming.

The endorsement of science notwithstanding, Ventura's valgus extension overload in late May raised concerns. Was this the breakdown coaches feared? Happily, the MRI results came back negative. After missing just one start, the right-hander returned on June 5th to pitch six strong innings in a victory. "Ace" Ventura was back on track. Royals Nation breathed a sigh of relief.

While Ventura was one of the youngest starting pitchers in the majors, the next hurler in the Royals rotation was closer to the other end of the spectrum. Graduating in 1997 as class valedictorian from Ashland High in Ashland, Oregon, **Jeremy Guthrie** attended college at Brigham Young. Finishing his freshman year with an ERA over 6.00 for a mediocre team, the 18-year-old felt burned out by baseball.

So he moved to Spain to serve as a Mormon missionary. Per Church requirements, he had to leave behind any distractions to his mission—his girlfriend, his chessboard, and his glove. Barely thinking about baseball in Spain, Guthrie was ready to abandon the game forever if that was God's plan for him. He recalled praying, "I'm going to give this up, and I know whatever happens will be the best for me and it will be thy will."

Upon his return to the States two years later, Guthrie enrolled at Stanford, where his path led back to the diamond. Making the baseball team as a walk on, he enjoyed playing again. He soon emerged as one of the nation's top collegiate pitchers. Cleveland selected him in the first round of the 2002 draft, but he lingered in the Indians farm system for the next four seasons. The right-hander made one start for Cleveland in 2006, before the organization released him.

Baltimore grabbed Guthrie as a waiver claim in the off-season. When the Orioles gave him the opportunity to start in the majors, he remained a fixture in their rotation for five seasons. But after Guthrie twice led the American League in losses, Baltimore traded him to Colorado in February 2012. When his ERA ballooned to 6.35, the Rockies shipped him to the Royals halfway through the season.

The change in scenery revitalized the much-traveled pitcher. He turned in a strong second half in 2012 and won 15 games for the Royals the following season. Heading into 2014, Guthrie provided a veteran, innings-eating, presence in Yost's rotation.

When **Danny Duffy** tossed seven scoreless innings at Chicago on June 14th, he became the fifth straight Royals starter to win a game. Of the five, Duffy represented the most recent addition to the rotation. This spot was instead slated for Bruce Chen, a veteran lefty who had won 44 games for the Royals from 2010-2013. But when a bulging disc sidelined Chen in early May, Yost needed a fifth starter.

As a senior at Cabrillo High School in Lompoc, California, Duffy attracted the interest of scouts with a fastball in the mid-90s and an ERA below 1.00. Like several of his Royals teammates, he was blessed with parents who supported his baseball ambitions. His father Dan, an investigator for the Santa Barbara County Sheriff's Department, coached his Little League teams. His mother Deanna spent money earned from her job at an elementary school to buy baseball equipment. A former softball player, Deanna also donned shin guards to catch her son's bullpen sessions.

Kansas City picked Duffy in the third round of the 2007 Draft, two rounds after the club had selected Mike Moustakas with its first pick. Duffy pitched well in the low minors, making the All-Star team for Class A Wilmington in 2009. The highly-regarded southpaw then shocked the organization by walking away from baseball during 2010 spring training.

After a couple months pondering his future, Duffy returned to the team in June. He wanted to play again. As Scott Sharp, Royals director of Minor League Operations, reported, "Danny took some time off to reassess his priorities and see if this was something he desired to do and realized he did." Duffy pitched well that season, reaching the Double-A level.

The young lefty began 2011 with the AAA Omaha Storm Chasers, before Kansas City called him up for his major league debut in May. Duffy made 20 starts for the Royals that year and had seemingly solidified his spot in the rotation. Only six starts into the 2012 season, however, he suffered a torn elbow ligament that required Tommy John surgery—a procedure that typically sidelines pitchers for a full year. After rehab starts for Northwest Arkansas and Omaha the summer of 2013, Duffy returned to the majors to start five games for Kansas City.

Though he did not make the rotation out of spring training in 2014, Royals coaches hoped the southpaw would play an important role in their bullpen. An injury to Chen changed these plans. Now Duffy had an important role to play as a starter.

TIGER HUNTING

A day after Duffy's gem against the White Sox, Shields labored through 110 pitches and 10 Chicago hits to pick up his eighth win of the year. Kansas City's winning streak reached seven games, pulling the team within a game and a half of the division-leading Tigers. And as scheduling fate would have it, KC next traveled to Detroit for a four-game series against the very team that had won all five contests against them this year.

Reversing this trend, the Royals exploded for 17 hits to capture the first game 11-8. Infante torched his old team for four RBI, three of them from a homer off former Cy Young winner Justin Verlander. Kansas City brought more thunder the second night, bludgeoning their Motor City hosts with 15 hits and 11 runs. Gordon and Moustakas clubbed two-run shots off reigning AL Cy Young-winner Max Scherzer to knock the Tigers out of first place for the first time all year. The Royals had not held a division lead this late in the season since 2003.

The next day Jeremy Guthrie and the bullpen pitched KC to a 2-1 victory, extending the team's lead to a game and a half. Even more exciting, the Royals had built a 10-game winning streak for the first time in 20 years, and just the fifth time in franchise history. Billy Butler, Jarrod Dyson, Alcides Escobar, and Salvador Perez had all hit better than .375 during the run, with the KC catcher riding a 12-game hitting streak.

Ten straight wins? Hitting streaks? First place? What in the name of Jamie Quirk was going on with these guys?

Duffy pitched well in the series finale in Motown, but the Royals lost 2-1 to end the streak. It had still been a great run, especially Kansas City's series victory against its chief rival. Optimism surged throughout Royals Nation as their division-leading team returned for a nine-game home stand.

And then reality came crashing down. Seattle swept three games at The K. The Los Angeles Dodgers arrived with ace Zack Greinke poised to extend the losing streak to five. Rising to the occasion, the Royals tagged their former Cy Young teammate with 11 hits to take the first game. But Los Angeles rebounded to seize the next two contests. After winning ten in a row, Kansas City had dropped six out of seven. And with Detroit starting to win again, the Boys in Blue had fallen four games out of first. Not since the French Revolution had a group of royals endured such a grisly week.

The Los Angeles Angels, winners of six straight, arrived in town hoping to continue this reign of terror at The K. Kansas City escaped the guillotine in Game 1 when Infante slugged a grand slam to propel the home team to victory. After LA took the second contest, Infante singled home the game winner in the series finale to save the monarchy for the time being. Kansas City next traveled to Minneapolis, where they bested the Twins in the series opener on June 30th.

It had been an exciting month for the Royals. Though some disappointing losses followed the streak, Yost's boys still posted a 17-10 record for June. Those are the type of numbers that keep a team in contention. Just past the halfway point in the 2014 season, Kansas City's record was 43-39.

If the Royals could match their strong second half from the previous season, things might get interesting.

Chapter 7

July: Building Confidence

The Royals opened the month of July with a blowout loss to Minnesota, evening the series 1-1. In the rubber game at Target Field, Jason Vargas tossed seven shutout innings to log his eighth win of the season.

The Royals flew to Cleveland, where they dropped two of three to the Tribe. Heading next to Tampa Bay, Kansas City rebounded to take two of three from the Rays. The team finished its nine-game road trip with a respectable 5-4 record, and trailed first-place Detroit by 4.5 games with four to play before the All-Star Break.

And guess who was coming to The K for a four-game set? The Detroit series represented a big opportunity. Sweeping the Tigers would draw the Royals to within a half-game of first and potentially spark a momentum shift that could alter the balance of power in the AL Central. Even taking three of four would make a strong statement before the break. Management hoped a new acquisition might help the team issue such a statement. This signee may have been a recent arrival in KC, but his relationship with the club extended back farther than any of the current regulars.

Kansas City signed free agent **Raul Ibanez** on June 30th. With right fielder Nori Aoki on the DL with a left groin strain,

Dayton Moore hoped the 42-year-old Ibanez, recently released by the Angels, would fill the lineup gap and provide another veteran presence in a clubhouse of youngsters. Adding to his appeal, the team's newest outfielder had a history with the Royals—he had been playing at The K when many of the current players were still in high school.

Ibanez was born in New York City in 1972, a year before Kauffman Stadium opened. A few years earlier, his father Juan Armando escaped with his family from communist Cuba. A chemist in his native country, Raul's father found employment as a warehouseman for a cruise ship company in the States. Leading by example, Juan Armando taught his son the value of hard work.

This ethic drove Ibanez even in his teenage years. Often times when driving home from baseball practice at Sunset High School in Miami, he would feel the urge to continue working on his swing. Stopping his car, he pulled out a bat, several worn baseballs, and an orange construction cone from the trunk. The young man then placed the balls on the cone like a tee and hit them into a fence. These impromptu batting sessions could last until nightfall.

Young Ibanez refined his skills as a catcher while following the tutelage of future big league manager Fredi Gonzalez, a backstop in the Yankees organization who worked security at his high school in the off-season. After graduating from Sunset High, Ibanez attended Miami-Dade Community College, where he played outfield and catcher. In June 1992 Seattle drafted the 20-year-old in the 36th round.

Though Ibanez was a good ballplayer, questions remained as to whether he had the talent needed to succeed at the big league level. He remained determined, despite his slow climb up the rungs of the Mariners farm system. In August 1996, Seattle called him to The Show, but just for a cup of coffee. For the next four seasons Ibanez split time between the Mariners and Triple-A Tacoma.

Following the 2000 campaign, Ibanez signed as a free agent with Kansas City. His playing time increasing, he logged his first hundred-game season in the majors in 2001. The following year, he became a fixture in the Royals lineup, topping 500 at-bats and 100 RBI for the first time as a big leaguer. In 2003 Ibanez batted .294 with 18 HRs and 90 RBI to help Kansas City finish with a winning record for the first time in nine years.

A free agent after the season, Ibanez signed with Seattle. The outfielder thrived in his return to the Pacific Northwest. From 2004-2008, Ibanez averaged 23 home runs and 98 RBI a season for the Mariners.

Having established himself as a productive lefty bat and a positive clubhouse presence, he signed a three-year $31.5 million deal with Philadelphia in December 2008. Ibanez shined in his first season in the National League, slugging 34 homers, making the All-Star team, and batting .304 in the World Series for the champion Phillies.

After three years in Philly, Ibanez signed with the Yankees. That October, he joined the list of Bronx Bombers with dramatic postseason hits on their resume. In the 2012 ALDS against Baltimore, Ibanez homered in the ninth to tie Game 2. In his next at bat, he cleared the fence in the twelfth to win the game for New York. At age 40, Ibanez became the oldest player to hit a postseason walk-off home run, as well as the first player to hit two homers in the ninth inning or later of a postseason game.

In 2013 Ibanez returned to Seattle, where he hit 29 home runs. The following season, he moved on to the Los Angeles Angels. After Ibanez's average dipped to .157, the Angels cut him in late June. Dayton Moore quickly seized the opportunity to bring a veteran leader back to the Royals clubhouse. On July 2nd, just two days after his signing, Ibanez homered in a KC victory over Minnesota.

On Thursday, July 10th, Kansas City hosted the first of four games against division-leading Detroit. Thus far in 2014 the Tigers owned a 6-3 advantage in head-to-head matchups. But the

Royals hoped to send a message that they were now contenders for the division crown. Instead, it was the Motor City madmen who did the talking. Or, more specifically, their bats. The Detroit lineup shelled Jeremy Guthrie in the opener, knocking him from the mound in the fifth. The KC bullpen fared no better as every Tiger batter recorded at least one hit and one run in the 16-4 pasting.

The next game settled into a pitchers' duel between Danny Duffy and Tigers starter Anibal Sanchez. Trailing 2-1 in the eighth, Kansas City threatened to tie the game against Joba Chamberlain, Alex Gordon's former teammate at Nebraska. After singling to lead off the inning, Nori Aoki stole second and advanced to third on an errant throw. That would have given the Royals the tying run at third with no outs, but the umpire called Lorenzo Cain for batter interference on the throw. Cain was out and Aoki had to return to first. Kansas City failed to score and ended up losing by one run.

The following night Detroit starter Rick Porcello shut down the Royals to win his AL-leading 12th game. Kansas City fell to 0-6 against the Tigers at home and dropped seven and a half games behind the division leaders. Though admitting his team had underachieved thus far in 2014, Ned Yost tried to remain optimistic. "We know we're a second-half club," the manager said. "We've been a second-half club."

In the final game before the All-Star Break, KC faced Justin Verlander and the prospect of a demoralizing four-game sweep at home. Back in the rotation due to Jason Vargas's appendectomy absence, Bruce Chen pitched into the sixth, surrendering only two runs. Kansas City then erupted for five in the seventh to take the lead. The bullpen made it hold up, giving KC a much-needed victory. After the disaster-averting win, the team headed into the break with a 48-46 record.

Though they still trailed Detroit by 6.5 games, the Royals players echoed their manager's hopes about the rest of the season. "We're just better the second half," said Billy Butler. "It's our track record and we're starting to count on it."

If the Royals were to make a move in the second half, they would need their running game to remain in high gear. The team stole four bases in the Detroit series to enter the All-Star Break with 79, best in the American League. Outfielder **Jarrod Dyson** accounted for 18 of those first-half thefts. Having coined the phrase *"that's what speed do,"* Dyson embodied one of Kansas City's most important advantages on the field.

As a young child, Dyson lived in the public-housing projects of McComb, Mississippi. Residents called the drug and violence-infested complex "The Bricks." When Dyson was eight, his mother Cecelia moved her five children to a safer side of town. Despite being blessed with athletic ability, Dyson drifted away from sports in middle school. His mother and a military man named Jerry Hill helped guide him back. Following the tutelage of Hill, who became a father figure, Dyson learned the game of baseball. He in fact learned well enough to star at McComb High School and Southwest Mississippi Community College.

Despite wheels that could leave a Ferrari in the dust, Dyson generated little excitement from major league scouts. In 2006 Kansas City selected him in the 50th round—the *very last* round—of the draft. Though picked after 1,474 other players, Dyson considered his selection a blessing. "[The Royals] saw something in me when I didn't see it in myself," the outfielder said. "I just thank them for everything they did for me."

Though nobody could question his speed, Dyson's lack of hitting limited his playing time during his first years in the minors. In the spring of 2009, he failed a drug test because of pain medication he had taken for a toothache. Suspended for 50 games, Dyson slipped perilously close to getting cut. When he resumed playing, his bat heated up and his stolen base totals climbed. In September 2010, he debuted in the majors as a late-season call-up.

After splitting time between Kansas City and Triple-A Omaha in 2011, Dyson emerged as an invaluable reserve for the Royals in 2012. With Cain missing time due to injury, Dyson played over 100 games, batted .260, and stole 30 bases. The following season, he spent a month on the DL with a sprained ankle after an ill-fated wall-climbing effort to rob Steve Trout of a home run. Despite the extended absence, the outfielder stole 34 bases in just 87 games.

Along the way, Dyson strived to improve his game— working the count, bunting, drawing walks, and hitting grounders. Absorbing wisdom from his Gold Glove teammate Alex Gordon, he improved his fielding as well. Though still a fourth outfielder heading into the 2014 season, Dyson was a vital cog in the Royals machine. Even when he did not start, Yost often tabbed him to pinch run or enter the game as a defensive replacement. Indeed, when Dyson and his acres-covering range joined Gordon and Cain in the field, Kansas City boasted arguably the best defensive outfield in all of baseball.

Even when not playing, Dyson made his presence known. With a mouth that could move faster than his legs, he needled his teammates with daily jabs and encouragements. Though his confident remarks to the media sometimes stirred the pot, the outfielder's levity helped keep things loose among the other Royals. Well aware of his loquacious reputation in the clubhouse, Dyson once wondered aloud, "What would it be like without me?" Teammate Lorenzo Cain replied, "Quiet."

ALL STARS

Historically, playing in a small market has left Royals players at a disadvantage in the All-Star Game balloting. In 2014 that trend continued as none of the Kansas City players topped the fan voting at their positions. Peer voting was a different story. American League players selected three Royals for the 2014 AL All-Star team: Alex Gordon, Salvador Perez, and Greg Holland. All three were making their second straight appearance in the Midsummer Classic.

Gordon was the best-known Royal on the national stage. Not since Willie Wilson in 1982-83 had a Royals outfielder appeared in two straight All-Star games. Heading into the break, Gordon was batting .268 with 9 home runs and 44 RBI. His sure-handed play in left field, meanwhile, continued his reign as one of the best defensive outfielders in the game.

In addition to his estimable work behind the plate, Perez delivered a .283 average with 11 home runs in the first half. An injury to Baltimore's Matt Wieters, the top vote-getter among AL catchers, meant Perez would be starting. Not since Jermaine Dye in 2000 had a Royals position player started an All-Star game.

Holland was the first Royals pitcher to gain back-to-back All-Star selections since Jeff Montgomery in 1992-93. With 25 saves, a 1.82 ERA, and nearly 14 strikeouts per nine innings, Holland had dominated in the first half. The closer praised his teammates for helping him achieve such success. "We were kind of hoping for a few more guys to join us," Holland said, "but it's special to be around Salvy, because he's helped me personally so much, and so has Gordo, diving and throwing guys out at the plate."

Gordon, unfortunately, would not appear in the Midsummer Classic. A sprained wrist that had shelved him for all four games against Detroit remained an issue. With a healthy return after the break the main priority, the outfielder had to sacrifice his opportunity to play in the All-Star Game. The Royals hoped the week-long layoff would be enough for Gordon to avoid a trip to the disabled list.

Played at Target Field in Minneapolis, the 85th All-Star Game marked a farewell celebration for New York shortstop Derek Jeter, who would retire at the end of the season. The Yankee captain got things started for the AL with a leadoff double in the first. After Mike Trout tripled him home, Miguel Cabrera drilled a homer to stake the Junior Circuit to a 3-0 lead. The National League later tied it, but Trout doubled in the go-ahead run in the fifth to give the American League a lead it would not relinquish.

Perez caught five innings and grounded out against Cy Young-winner Clayton Kershaw in his one at-bat. Holland entered the game in the seventh with the AL leading 5-3. Despite roiling nerves, he needed only nine pitches to send the NL down in order, preserving his team's lead.

Victory in the All-Star Game meant the American League pennant winner would have home field advantage in the World Series. Games 1 and 2 and Games 6 and 7, if necessary, would be played at the AL champion's ballpark. But did that really matter to the Royals, sitting just two games above .500? From the perspective of July 15th, few, if any, baseball experts believed Kauffman Stadium would be hosting World Series games in October.

DOG DAYS OF SUMMER

After four days off, Kansas City resumed play in Boston on Friday, July 18th. The schedule-makers seemed to have provided a gift by allowing the Royals to open the second half against the last place Red Sox. Even more good news arrived with Alex Gordon's return to the lineup. But then came the bad news— Boston roughed up Shields to take the series opener 5-4.

Worse news followed. Kansas City scored only one run over the next two games to drop all three contests at Fenway. The team limped to Chicago, where its offense remained cold in a series-opening 3-1 loss. Yost's so-called "second-half club" had stumbled to four straight losses after the All-Star Break. The team fell into third place with a mediocre 48-50 record—eight games behind the Tigers.

And the figurative rain threatened to become a downpour in the Windy City. Hosmer had to sit out the series opener due to a hand contusion suffered in Boston. Perez did not catch because of a groin strain. Moustakas did not start at third because his .190 batting average offered little chance of success against White Sox lefty Chris Sale. What was supposed to be a breakthrough season for Kansas City started to circle the drain.

The next day, July 22nd, the oldest Royal called a players-only team meeting in the visiting locker room at U.S. Cellular Field. In an impassioned speech, Raul Ibanez told his younger teammates they had incredible talent and potential. He could see it when he had played for the Angels weeks earlier. Kansas City's opponents could see it too. The Royals just needed to believe it themselves.

Ibanez's words had an impact. Alex Gordon said he and his teammates came out of the meeting feeling much different about themselves. But would these good feelings matter on the diamond?

That night Kansas City erupted for 14 hits in a 7-1 triumph to end their slide. Moustakas blasted two homers on, appropriately enough, Greek Heritage Night at the ballpark. As for the inspiring old man, Ibanez punctuated his earlier oration with two hits, including a double and an RBI.

Kansas City won again the next day to take the series against the Chi-Sox. The Royals returned to The K for a four-game set against Cleveland. Nori Aoki singled home the winning run in the fourteenth inning to claim the opener. After taking the next two from the Tribe, Kansas City's winning streak reached five.

The team had not lost since Ibanez's speech. Coincidence? Not according to the players. "We were on a downhill track," James Shields said. "We needed to believe in ourselves again. He [Ibanez] gave us that confidence we were missing." Dyson concurred. "We were on that slippery slope, but Raul now has everybody in here believing in each other, believing in their ability, and believing we can get it done."

The Royals dropped the series finale against Cleveland, then took two of three from the Twins to finish July with a 55-52 mark. Kansas City had reclaimed second place and closed to within four games of division-leading Detroit. The team remained in contention with just two months left in the season.

The end of July marks the non-waiver trade deadline in the major leagues. This is a time when contenders try to add an impact player or two to increase their chances for a playoff berth and a deep run in the postseason. At the same time, teams that have fallen out of the race seek to unload high-priced soon-to-be free agents. This confluence of motivated buyers and sellers usually results in many transactions the last week of July.

Most years the Royals were among those teams unloading expensive veterans for talented prospects. But this time, with a playoff spot still within reach, Dayton Moore looked to upgrade his roster. Earlier in the month the GM hoped to make a deal to acquire Tampa Bay ace David Price, the 2012 Cy Young winner. Signs were pointing the right way until KC had to back out due to the huge $17 million salary Price would command. Seizing the opportunity, Detroit swooped in and snatched Price.

Kansas City targeted other big names, but again could not afford the price tag. And so the trade deadline passed without the Royals adding a big name. Making matters worse, the team they were trying to catch bolstered its already fearsome rotation with yet another ace. Although disappointed, Kansas City's players tried to remain focused on winning games. "There's nothing we can do about it," said Gordon, commenting on the Tigers acquisition of Price. "It just means we've got to beat one more Cy Young winner in that rotation."

Though they failed to make a big splash, the Royals were not completely inactive on the trade market. On July 28th they sent reserve infielder Danny Valencia to Toronto for catcher Erik Kratz and minor league pitcher Liam Hendricks. In making this deal, Moore hoped for an offensive upgrade at the second-string catcher spot. Perez's backup to this point, Brett Hayes, had been hitting an anemic .135.

Before joining the Royals in December 2013, the 29-year-old Valencia had played for three different major league teams since his rookie campaign in 2010. A useful utility man for Kansas City, he had filled in at second when Infante was injured and played third when Yost wanted to sit Moustakas against a lefty starter. Valencia had hit .282 in 110 at-bats in 2014 before the trade.

To fill Valencia's absence, Kansas City recalled Christian Colon from Omaha. The Royals first-round draft pick in 2010, Colon had batted .310/.366/.432 in the minors in 2014 prior to his promotion. The 25-year-old Puerto Rican infielder played second base, third base, and shortstop, providing Yost with a versatile backup when he wanted to rest one of his regulars. During a brief stint with the Royals earlier in the season, Colon showed his potential by slamming three extra base hits in a victory over the Indians.

These late July bench moves notwithstanding, the Royals would play the final two months of the season with largely the same roster. And that was not necessarily a bad thing. Sometimes making no move is the right move. Many a team has gutted its farm system, parting ways with a future superstar mid-season to add a veteran who did not pan out. In 2000, for example, Toronto approached the trade deadline in a tight race for the AL East title. Seeking an impact arm, the Blue Jays acquired pitcher Esteban Loaiza from Texas in exchange for prospect Michael Young. Loaiza went 5-7 in the second half for Toronto, which failed to make the playoffs. Young, on the other hand, became one of the best infielders in baseball over the next decade, appearing in seven All-Star Games for the Rangers.

Contrary to the railings of various commentators, Moore's lack of activity at the end of July should not have been interpreted as a season-killing failure. More troubling, however, was the team's persisting inconsistency. Kansas City finished July with a 12-13 record. On the plus side though, the Royals did improve in the latter part of the month after Ibanez's speech. Time would tell if this inspired play would continue long term or wither in the August heat.

Chapter 8

August: Catching Fire

The Royals opened the new month on the West Coast, where they faced Oakland in a three-game series. If Kansas City made the playoffs, the first-place A's loomed as a possible barrier to the pennant. Like the Tigers, Oakland had recently concluded a blockbuster trade deadline deal to land a top-of-the-rotation starter—Red Sox ace Jon Lester.

One key Royal would not be making the trip west. After aggravating his hand on a check swing a day earlier, Eric Hosmer went in for X-rays. The results showed a fractured finger on his right hand. The first baseman had actually sustained the injury ten days prior when hit by a Jon Lester pitch in Boston. Thinking it was just a contusion, Hosmer tried to play through it. With the fracture, however, he would miss the next month.

For the series opener Kansas City would face Oakland's Sonny Gray, who had already won 12 games this season. As good as advertised, the young starter cooled off the Royal bats, limiting the visitors to one run. Fortunately, Guthrie and the KC bullpen were even better, shutting out the A's for a 1-0 victory.

Though Kansas City tagged Lester for nine hits the next day, Oakland scored eight runs in the fifth inning to claim the second contest at O.co Coliseum. In the rubber game, the Royals

82

ripped 14 hits to support Shields, who won his 10th game of the season. Yost's boys next traveled to Arizona, where they outscored the home team 22-7 in a three-game sweep over the Diamondbacks.

On Friday, August 8th, the Royals returned home for seven straight games at The K. The first three would be interleague contests against the San Francisco Giants. Billy Butler got his team off to a fast start in the opening tilt with a two-run homer in the first inning. After the Giants later tied it, Butler drove in the go-ahead run with a single in the sixth. Gordon added an insurance RBI and KC prevailed 4-2. Though on the losing end, San Francisco's starter threw 123 pitches in a complete game. His name: Madison Bumgarner.

The following evening brought a multitude of fans from Nebraska for Husker Night at The K. Shields dominated the visitors with a four-hit shutout. The red-clad spectators received an additional treat when former Cornhusker Alex Gordon homered in the fifth. The next afternoon the Royals handed out Gordon bobbleheads. The left fielder responded with another home run, as 10,000 of his bobbling likenesses nodded their approval. Gordon's teammates stole seven bases to help the Royals thwart former Cy Young-winner Tim Lincecum.

The sweep of the Giants gave Kansas City a seven-game winning streak. With a 64-53 record the team had closed to within a half-game of division-leading Detroit, which had inexplicably fallen into a slump despite its Cy Young-laden rotation. On August 11th Oakland arrived for a four-game set at The K. Kansas City won the first contest 3-2 to grab a half-game lead in the division. After catching the final out, Jarrod Dyson kept an earlier promise to his teammates by performing a backflip. Billy Butler did not try to match him.

Adding to the excitement of this week was the presence of a special guest from halfway around the world. SungWoo Lee first encountered the Royals in the mid-1990s when he watched sports highlight shows in South Korea to improve his English. Enamored with the Royals' beautiful stadium, he soon became a

Kansas City fan. Seeking to learn more about the team, SungWoo studied Royals lore. Though day games aired at 3:00 a.m. in South Korea, he got up in the middle of the night to watch his beloved team. With diehard loyalty even through the lean years, SungWoo became arguably the Royals biggest fan in the Eastern Hemisphere.

Social media allowed SungWoo to correspond with his blue-clad counterparts in the United States. When he posted on Twitter his plans to visit Kansas City to watch his favorite team, a welcoming campaign quickly grew. Royals fans formed a committee to chauffer him around town. He toured Kauffman Stadium and received Royals attire and souvenirs, including a customized "SungWoo Lee" jersey. He met the players and Ned Yost, as well as Royals legends George Brett and Frank White. The team's undefeated run since SungWoo's arrival in the States on August 5th added to his celebrity status. The crowd at The K roared when he appeared on the stadium video screen. Their delight increased when the "Superfan" threw out the first pitch for the series opener against Oakland. SungWoo departed for South Korea a few days later.

He would return to Kansas City sooner than he realized.

THE THREE-HEADED MONSTER

While Royals fans had fun speculating that the team's recent hot streak stemmed from the good luck brought by SungWoo, the team's opponents knew there was something more ominous behind the blue resurgence. It was not the Royal bats that gave opposing managers nightmares. Lorenzo Cain was the only KC regular batting over .300 at the time, and Kansas City was last in the majors in home runs. Instead, what made the Royals so terrifying was a three-headed beast that dwelled in the bullpen lair beyond the left field fence at Kauffman Stadium.

Relievers Kelvin Herrera, Wade Davis, and Greg Holland (aka H-D-H) pitched three scoreless innings in Kansas City's 3-2 victory over Oakland on August 11th. It had become a familiar formula for the Boys in Blue. If Kansas City held a lead after six innings, the game nearly always ended with a Royals victory. Each member of the H-D-H trio would finish the season with 60-plus innings and an ERA below 1.50. Given that no MLB team ever had three relievers accomplish that feat in the same season, many experts argued that the 2014 Royals had the best bullpen in baseball history.

In the summer of 2006, new Royals GM Dayton Moore escalated the team's scouting efforts in international markets, especially Latin America. Moore tabbed former Braves scout Rene Francisco to head the campaign. Later that year Francisco and his scouts discovered a Dominican teenager with a wicked fastball. They wasted little time signing the young man. His name: **Kelvin Herrera**.

After a season in the Dominican Summer League, Herrera pitched for Burlington in the Appalachian circuit in 2008. The kid's heat and 1.42 ERA earned him a promotion from Rookie level to Class A by the end of the season. But an elbow stress fracture shelved Herrera for most of the 2009 and 2010 seasons. The young hurler wondered if his career was over. "I was only twenty-one years old," he said, "and I was scared even though the doctors told me it would eventually get better."

Herrera moved to the bullpen in 2011 to ease the strain on his elbow. This shift, along with the 25 pounds he added to his frame, worked wonders. His velocity and strikeouts increased, while his ERA plummeted. Herrera rapidly climbed the farm system ladder to Triple-A Omaha, where he posted a 2.12 ERA in 17 innings. Though his control remained a concern, some coaches believed he had the stuff to be a future closer in the majors. Kansas City gave him a taste of The Show in late September.

Herrera and his blazing fastball made the big league roster out of spring training in 2012. The rookie did not disappoint. As a key setup man in Yost's bullpen, he struck out 77 batters in 84 innings, while delivering a 2.35 ERA and three saves. The

85

following spring, however, Herrera took a step backwards. Batters launched his offerings over the fence with alarming frequency, inflating his ERA to almost 5.00. In May management sent him to the minors to work on keeping the ball in the park. As with several of his teammates, the time in Omaha helped. Herrera returned in June a far more effective pitcher. He surrendered only one home run the rest of the season.

In 2014 Herrera developed an effective curveball to accompany his fastballs that could hit 101-mph on the radar gun. Early that summer, Yost worked out a plan for how to deploy his pitchers each game. His starter would ideally go six innings. If ahead on the scoreboard, the bullpen could handle the final three frames. And the seventh inning belonged to Herrera.

After the seventh, Kansas City's opponents had to face the second head of the Royals bullpen monster. **Wade Davis** grew up in Lake Wales, a small town in central Florida. As a youth, Davis and his stepbrother Dustin Huguley hunted and fished in the nearby swamps. The pair also spent hours on the diamond— Davis pitched and Huguley was his catcher. Davis became a star hurler in high school, attracting scouts and media attention. Retaining a humility instilled by his father Ben, the young pitcher insisted that any photographs for stories about him include his teammates as well.

During his senior season, Davis planned to attend the University of Florida—part of a recruiting class that included Billy Butler. Also interested in the right-hander, Tampa Bay selected Davis in the third round of the 2004 draft. With a $475,000 signing bonus on the table, Davis changed his plans to become a Gator, just as Butler had done.

After a shaky Rookie League campaign, Davis rose through the Tampa Bay farm system. He logged an impressive 33-19 mark in the minors from 2007-2009 to emerge as one of the Rays most promising pitching prospects. Claiming a spot in manager Joe Maddon's 2010 rotation, Davis went 12-10 with a 4.07 ERA—numbers that garnered a fourth-place finish in the

AL Rookie of the Year voting. After another solid season as a starter, Davis moved to the bullpen in 2012. The young pitcher thrived in middle relief, lowering his ERA to 2.43.

That December Tampa Bay included Davis in a multiplayer deal with Kansas City. The headliners in the trade were Rays ace James Shields and star Royals prospect Wil Myers. Davis was something of an afterthought in Dayton Moore's much-criticized transaction.

Kansas City acquired Davis with the idea of moving him back to the starting rotation. Now accustomed to his role as a reliever, the Florida right-hander dreaded the adjustment. Hits rocketed off opposing bats and his ERA soared. A tough season got worse in August when Davis received word that his stepbrother and childhood friend Dustin Huguley had died at age 25 from a congenital heart defect. In the offseason, Davis changed his jersey number to 17, the number Huguley wore for his high school baseball team.

In 2014 the Royals lost Luke Hochevar to injury in spring training. Yost needed a new setup reliever. He chose Davis as his eighth-inning man. The decision proved to be a stroke of genius. Thriving in his return to the bullpen, Davis became nearly untouchable. He averaged more than a strikeout per inning and his ERA remained below 1.00 through mid-August. The afterthought in the Shields-Myers trade had become one of the most dominant relievers in baseball.

After facing Herrera and Davis, life for opposing batters did not get any easier in the ninth inning. For that is when **Greg Holland**, the third head of KC's bullpen monster, bared his fangs. As a boy, Holland spent summers outdoors with his brother Chase tossing a football, hunting deer, and fishing near their trailer park in rural Marion, North Carolina. Young Holland learned to appreciate these outdoor opportunities growing up in the foothills of the Blue Ridge Mountains. The lad also picked up a strong drive to succeed from his dad Scott and mom Kim.

"Anything worth doing, is worth doing to the best of your ability," his carpenter father told him.

Holland would draw upon this philosophy as an undersized 150-pound infielder in high school. Despite his lack of stature, he remained determined. "I just wanted to compete and see how far I could push myself and how good a player I could be," he said. Holland occasionally took the mound in high school, but his size and a broken jaw limited his innings. Few colleges showed interest, despite his .370 senior year batting average. After graduating, he attended Western Carolina University, where he made the baseball team as a walk-on.

Noting his work habits and velocity, the WCU coaches groomed Holland as a pitcher. Following the instruction of Catamount pitching coach Paul Menhart, the young right-hander improved his mechanics. The once diminutive prep infielder bulked up into a fireballing all-conference closer by his junior year of college. Kansas City selected Holland in the 10th Round of the 2007 draft—the same draft they selected Mike Moustakas.

At first the Royals were not sure if Holland was best suited as a reliever or part of the future rotation. After starting seven games at Class A Wilmington in 2008, he moved exclusively to the bullpen the next year. Following a solid 2010 season in Omaha, he became a fixture in the Kansas City bullpen in 2011. As Joakim Soria's setup man, Holland thrived his rookie year with a 1.80 ERA. Ever determined, the young North Carolinian dreamed about closing for KC. "I knew if I could throw the eighth inning and be successful," Holland recalled, "why couldn't I come in in the ninth and be successful?"

He would get his opportunity the next season, when the Royals traded Soria's successor, Jonathan Broxton, to Cincinnati in July. In 2013, his first full season as Kansas City's closer, Holland set a franchise record with 47 saves. He struck out 103 batters in just 67 innings, while posting a minuscule 1.21 ERA. This performance earned him a spot on the All-Star team and a ninth-place finish in the AL Cy Young voting.

The following spring, the Royals closer picked up where he left off. His 2014 campaign was just as impressive as the previous year. If Greg Holland entered the game, a Kansas City victory was likely three outs away.

Their series-opening victory against the A's on August 11th gave the Royals an eight-game winning streak. Unfortunately this run ended the following night at the hands of Oakland's new ace Jon Lester. Kansas City rebounded to take the next two, winning a key series against a potential playoff opponent.

The less-heralded bullpen trio of Aaron Crow, Jason Frasor and Francisley Bueno recorded four important outs in the series finale victory. A first-round pick in 2009, Crow made the AL All-Star team two years later during a splendid rookie campaign. Though his fastball lost velocity and his ERA climbed late in 2014, he had served as a viable weapon out of the pen through the first half of the season. Kansas City had acquired Frasor in a mid-July trade with Texas, adding a veteran right-hander to Yost's middle relief corps. After this change of employers, Frasor pitched with better control and a lower ERA. Bueno had lost nearly two months earlier in the 2014 season to a sprained finger. Following his return in June, he provided situational value when Yost wanted a southpaw to face a left-handed batter in the late innings.

On August 15th, the first-place Royals traveled to Minneapolis to start a nine-game road trip. Taking three of four from the Twins, Kansas City boosted its division lead to two games. The team, moreover, had won its eighth straight series, a feat not achieved by a KC squad since 1991. Flying to Colorado on August 19th, the Royals helped manager Ned Yost celebrate his 59th birthday with a 7-4 victory over the Rockies. After losing the next night to split the two-game set in Denver, Kansas City headed to Texas. The Royals defeated the Rangers 6-3 in the opening game, behind a homer and two runs scored by Josh Willingham. Acquired eleven days earlier in a trade with Minnesota, the 35-year-old slugger had hit at least 24 home runs in a season for four different teams. With Billy Butler covering first during Hosmer's absence, Willingham provided a veteran power bat to platoon with Ibanez at DH.

The Royals won the second contest in Arlington by an identical 6-3 score. The victories against Texas gave red hot Kansas City 19 wins in its last 23 games. Now boasting a 72-56 record, the Boys in Blue had extended their lead in the AL Central to a season-high three games. With only 34 left to play, the Royals actually had a magic number. A playoff spot was not only a possibility, it was starting to look likely.

Although Texas prevailed in the series finale, it had still been a successful road trip for Kansas City. The team would play its next ten games at The K. First up were the Yankees in a makeup game that had been rained out in June. In his final appearance at Kauffman Stadium, Derek Jeter drove in two to help New York cruise 8-1. The loss trimmed the Royals division lead to a game and a half.

With the Twins arriving in town, Kansas City wanted to win the first contest to avoid a three-game skid. Surprisingly enough, Minnesota starter Ricky Nolasco was not on board with this plan. Shutting down the Royal bats, he yielded only three hits in seven innings. Heading into the bottom of the ninth, Kansas City trailed 1-0. Twins closer Glen Perkins came on for the save.

Leading off the final inning, Alcides Escobar blooped a single into right. Alex Gordon stepped into the batter's box. Like Robert Redford in *The Natural*, Gordon launched a drive over the right field wall for a dramatic walk-off victory (though without the exploding lights). His teammates rushed the field to celebrate an important win in the midst of a pennant race. Yost similarly was pleased, yet one detail about the night annoyed him. With only 13,847 fans at The K, the skipper spoke his mind afterwards. "We've been working hard to try to make our fans happy and make our fans proud of us for a lot of years," he said, "and we'd like them out here to enjoy a night like this with us, because this was a special night." The comments did little to improve the manager's tenuous approval rating with fans and the media.

Kansas City staged another late comeback the following night to win again. After Minnesota claimed the series finale, Cleveland arrived for the final three games of August. With a strong finish, the Royals could exceed 20 wins in a month for just the fifth time in franchise history. Instead, the Indians took the first two games and led the third contest 4-2 in the tenth when rain halted play. The game would resume three weeks later when the teams played their last scheduled series.

Despite the late stumble against Cleveland, Kansas City had torched its opponents for a 19-9 mark in August—the team's most wins in a month since 1989. With a 74-61 record, the Royals still led the division by a half game.

One month remained in the season.

Chapter 9

September: Battling to the Wire

Kansas City entered September with its best chance to make the postseason since 2003. That year, Tony Pena's Royals faded down the stretch, struggling to the finish line with a 13-15 record during the month. Would Yost's boys do the same, or would this year be different?

On September 1st, Labor Day, KC opened a three-game series against the Rangers. Yordano Ventura pitched into the seventh before the Three-Headed Monster nailed down a 4-3 victory. The next night, with the game tied in the eighth, Jarrod Dyson stole two bases to reach third with two outs. Salvador Perez's infield hit sent him home with the game-winning run. In Game 3, Alex Gordon homered to back a victorious outing from Jason Vargas. With the sweep, Kansas City remained in sole possession of first place in the AL Central.

After an off day, the Royals traveled to the Bronx for a three-game set against their longtime nemesis. Still in the hunt for a Wild Card spot, the Yankees especially wanted to make the playoffs in Derek Jeter's final season. Big Game James lived up to his moniker in the opener by shutting down the Bombers through 8.1 innings. Wade Davis finished off the 1-0 victory. After New York took Game 2, Ventura and the bullpen shut out the Yankees again in the series finale. With a two-game lead over Detroit, Kansas City eyed its first division crown since 1985.

Winning five of their first six games in September was not the only good news for the Royals. With teams allowed to expand their rosters from 25 to 40 players on the first of the month, reinforcements from the farm system had arrived in Kansas City. The most notable September addition to the Royals was actually not a minor leaguer, but a veteran coming back from injury. The return of Eric Hosmer added another impact bat to the lineup and a defensive upgrade at first. Butler had done a decent job fielding over the past month, but Hosmer brought Gold Glove-caliber defense to the position.

Roster expansion means different things to different franchises. Teams out of contention typically give their top farm prospects playing time in September to find out if they are ready for the next level. Kansas City usually fell into this category. But not in 2014. For contenders like the Royals this season, roster expansion was a time to add young talent that could play a key role in pushing their team into the postseason.

In June, just three months earlier, **Brandon Finnegan** toed the rubber for the Texas Christian University Horned Frogs in the College World Series. That same month, Kansas City selected the lefty as its first-round draft pick. Brandishing a mid-90s fastball, a hard-breaking slider, and a deceptive fading change-up, the 21-year-old blazed through Class A batters in July. By August Finnegan had climbed to AA Northwest Arkansas. Royals scouts liked the southpaw's dynamic stuff, projecting him as a future starter for KC. Seeking another weapon for the parent team's stretch drive, Dayton Moore and Ned Yost had more immediate plans for the youngster. Though such rapid advancement is not common nowadays, they promoted fresh-out-of-college Finnegan to the majors on September 1st. A few days later he made his debut against New York. Unfazed by the drama of pitching in the Big Apple, the kid tossed two shutout innings against the Bronx Bombers, with no hits, no walks, and two strikeouts.

While Finnegan made it to The Show because of his arm, a second notable call-up joined the Royals because of his legs. Kansas City selected **Terrance Gore** in the 20th round of the 2011 draft. As a teenager Gore starred on the football field in Gray, Georgia, where his coaches clocked his 40-yard-dash time at a blazing 4.29. Since his size (5' 7", 165 pounds) made him a longshot for an NFL career, the speedster focused on baseball. Burning up the base paths in junior college, he once scored all the way from first base on a wild pickoff throw. Though Gore struggled at the plate in the Royals farm system, he continued to run wild, stealing 68 bases for Class A Lexington in 2013. The following summer, KC coaches envisioned Gore as a pinch-running specialist. After his call-up, the speedster worked with first base coach Rusty Kuntz on how to steal against big league pitchers. "G. Baby," as his teammates called him, gave Yost a valuable weapon that could change a game without even picking up a bat.

Another late addition to the Royals was Jayson Nix, claimed off waivers from the Pirates. Though he was batting just .133 on the season, the veteran Nix could play second, short, and third, providing a versatile glove to bolster the team's infield depth. Kansas City also called up outfielders Carlos Peguero and Lane Adams, catcher Francisco Pena, infielder Johnny Giavotella, and pitchers Casey Coleman and Liam Hendriks. Later in the month, Kansas City recalled lefty reliever Tim Collins from Omaha.

The Royals would have little time to celebrate their series victory over the Yankees. The next day they flew to Detroit for a three-game set against the team that had owned them this season; the team chasing them for the division lead; the team that boasted a starting rotation with the last three AL Cy Young winners. Tigers manager Brad Ausmus called it the biggest series of the season. On that point, there would be little disagreement from the players in blue.

Royal bats came alive in the series opener at Comerica Park, led by Hosmer's three hits and Cain's inside-the-park home run. Unfortunately, that would not be enough. The Tigers pounded out eight hits and six runs in the third inning, en route to a 9-5 victory. Kansas City's division lead shriveled to a game and a half.

Detroit jumped out to an early 3-0 lead to support Max Scherzer in the second contest. Alex Gordon just missed a game-tying homer in the fifth, when his drive down the right field line hooked foul. Tiger closer Joe Nathan picked off Jarrod Dyson to escape a ninth-inning jam and preserve a 4-2 victory for the home team. In the first two games, the normally sure-handed Royals had committed four errors.

Facing the prospect of a devastating three-game sweep, James Shields took the hill for the series finale. Big Game James again showed up, limiting the Tigers to just two hits through seven scoreless innings. With Greg Holland sitting out due to triceps tightness, Herrera and Davis pitched the final two innings to finish the shutout. Kansas City hung onto first place.

Though they again took some lumps in the Motor City, the Royals survived. The division still very much within their grasp, the team headed home for ten straight games at The K. With Danny Duffy out due to shoulder soreness, Yost handed the ball to Liam Hendriks for the series opener against the Red Sox. Three errors from the KC infield helped Boston build a 4-2 lead after four innings. Aside from Cain's RBI single in the sixth, the Royals mounted little offense the rest of the way in a losing effort.

Kansas City mustered only four hits the next night to fall again to the BoSox. With his team in desperate need of a win, Jeremy Guthrie came through in the third game by tossing eight masterful innings. Finnegan pitched a scoreless ninth to close out a 7-1 victory. Kansas City jumped out to an early 4-0 in the finale—the big blast coming from Hosmer's three-run homer. But Boston battled back, taking the lead on Daniel Nava's grand slam. Unable to rally, KC lost for the third time in four tries against the last place Red Sox. The team's 2-5 slide had dropped them a game behind the Tigers in the AL Central. The Royals still led in the Wild Card race, but recent events jeopardized that possibility as well.

The next night, the White Sox visited The K and slammed Shields for ten hits. Disaster loomed as Chicago held a 3-0 lead after six. Kansas City narrowed the margin to 3-2 heading into the bottom of the ninth. After a one-out double by Mike Moustakas, pinch runner Dyson stole third and scored the tying run on a wild pitch. Following a two-out double by Nori Aoki, his fourth hit of the game, Yost sent in Gore to pinch run. The next batter, Cain, chopped a ball over the pitcher and sprinted up the line to barely beat out an infield hit. Gore meanwhile dashed around third to score the winning run. Kansas City had snatched a crucial victory from the jaws of defeat.

The following night, Chicago scored on both Herrera and Davis to tag KC's bullpen with a rare loss. In the rubber game, Royal bats came alive to back a stellar outing from Yordano Ventura, who picked up his 13th win of the season. Kansas City bagged a badly-needed series victory to remain just a game behind Detroit.

In the three games against Chicago, Royals right fielder **Nori Aoki** put on a batting clinic by rapping 11 base hits in 13 at-bats, plus two walks. His eleven hits broke a franchise record for a three-game series shared by George Brett and Willie Wilson. "He's hotter than a firecracker," Yost said. "You can't explain it."

Aoki was born in 1982 in Hyūga, Japan. After playing outfield for Waseda University, he debuted in Nippon Professional Baseball—Japan's highest league—in 2004 with the Yakult Swallows. In eight seasons with the Swallows, Aoki delivered an impressive .329 career batting average. Along the way, he won three Central League batting titles and became the only player in Japanese professional baseball to tally two 200-hit seasons. These batting numbers led many American scouts to label him the next Ichiro Suzuki—the Japanese hitting sensation who topped the American League in hitting seven times for Seattle between 2001 and 2010.

In December 2011, Milwaukee paid Yakult $2.5 million for the right to negotiate a contract with Aoki. After signing with the Brewers, the outfielder batted .287 with 50 stolen bases over a two-season span in 2012-13. Prior to the 2014 campaign, Milwaukee traded Aoki to Kansas City for Will Smith (a southpaw reliever, not the Fresh Prince of Bel-Air). Dayton Moore envisioned his acquisition as KC's new leadoff hitter. "With Nori at the top of the lineup, putting pressure on the defense and getting on base certainly improves our offense," the GM said.

Though he hit well in April, Aoki slumped through much of the first half of the 2014 season. Heading into the All-Star break, his batting average languished at .260. Hampered by a sore arm and a groin injury that landed him on the disabled list, Aoki's defense also underwhelmed. Working with Rusty Kuntz improved his outfield positioning, and his bat heated up in the second half. Following his three-day barrage against the White Sox, Aoki's batting average climbed to .283.

Just a few days earlier, Yost had dropped Aoki from leadoff to the second spot behind Alcides Escobar. The move was reminiscent of when Dick Howser switched Willie Wilson and Lonnie Smith at the top of his order late in the 1985 season. Howser's decision contributed to a world championship. Aoki's early results from the number-two spot suggested that Yost's decision might work out as well.

After taking two of three from the White Sox, Kansas City sat just a half-game back in the AL Central. The team was tied with Oakland for the first Wild Card spot and held a two-game lead over Seattle for the second Wild Card. Chances for a postseason berth were looking good, but a familiar nemesis was headed to town. Thus far this season the Royals had lost 11 out of 16 games to Detroit. That included a 1-6 mark at Kauffman Stadium, where the next three games would be played.

With playoff anticipation in western Missouri reaching levels not seen since the days of Brett, fans packed the ballpark for the series opener on Friday night. Some observers labeled the three-game set the most important games for Kansas City since the '85 World Series. Detroit sent its veteran ace Justin Verlander to the mound. KC countered with 11-game winner Jason Vargas. It was September 19th and the Royals were playing baseball that mattered.

Tigers second baseman Ian Kinsler led off the game with a single. Things got worse from there. Detroit led 3-0 after one inning. They knocked out Vargas in the fourth; by the end of that frame every Tiger in the starting lineup had at least one hit. The mauling continued after Royals relievers Casey Coleman and Louis Coleman entered the game. When the carnage finally ended, Detroit had pounded out 19 hits in a 10-1 blowout. The gap between the two AL Central rivals was just a game and a half, but it seemed a lot wider.

The next afternoon James Shields battled Max Scherzer in a pitcher's duel that turned on a bizarre play. With the game tied at one in the sixth, the Royals put baserunners on second and third with one out. Omar Infante lined out to Kinsler, but the Tiger second baseman threw wildly into left field trying to double-up Hosmer at second. Salvador Perez jogged home with what appeared to be the go-ahead run. But someone in the Detroit dugout noticed that Perez did not go back and touch third after Kinsler's catch. When the Tigers threw to third for an appeal, the umpires conferred. With the video board replay clearly showing that Perez did not make a valid tag up, the umps called him out. The game remained tied. Detroit pushed across two runs against Shields in the seventh, and held on to win 3-2.

Kansas City fell two and a half games back in the division and held just a half-game lead over Seattle for the second Wild Card spot. With one contest left against the Motor City persecutors, a playoff berth for the Royals was in jeopardy.

Getting swept at home by the Tigers could easily spiral into a full-blown September collapse that would extend Kansas City's postseason futility yet another year.

On Sunday afternoon, September 21st, fans packed The K for the final home game of the regular season. Home attendance for 2014 hit 1,915,482, the highest total for the franchise since 1991. The Boys in Blue brought the crowd to its feet early by breaking out to a 2-0 lead. Detroit tied it with runs in the third and fourth. Red hot Nori Aoki put the Royals on top again with a two-run triple. Jeremy Guthrie pitched effectively into the sixth, before turning it over to the bullpen. The Three-Headed Monster tamed the Tigers to close out a much-needed 5-2 win. "Today's game shows that we're not going away," Ned Yost said. Time would tell if the manager was right.

Seven games remained in the Royals season. All of them would be played on the road—three at Cleveland and then four at Chicago against the White Sox. Kansas City trailed Detroit by a game and a half in the division, and led Seattle by the same margin for a Wild Card spot. Though they would not get to see their team try to break the playoff drought at The K, Royals fans across the Heartland could watch the games on FOX Sports Kansas City with Ryan Lefebvre, Steve Physioc, and Rex Hudler calling the action. And just as he had been doing for 45 years, Denny Matthews delivered the play-by-play descriptions to the Royals radio audience.

Before the first game of the Cleveland series, Kansas City had to settle some unfinished business. The Indians-Royals game on August 31st had been suspended due to rain with Cleveland leading 4-2 in the 10th. Batting as the home team in the bottom of that inning, KC pushed across a run but fell short. The Wild Card lead shrunk by a half game.

With a playoff berth hanging in the balance, Danny Duffy weaved six shutout innings against the Tribe in the series opener. The bullpen continued the zeroes and Kansas City prevailed 2-0. Royal bats exploded for 13 hits the following night to back

Yordano Ventura, who baffled the Indians with his 100-mph heat. KC moved one step closer.

Though the Royals slammed ten more hits in the series finale, they fell 6-4 to Cleveland. Despite this disappointment, Kansas City had won an important late-season series. The team headed to Chicago for the final four games of the regular season. They trailed Detroit by two games in the AL Central, but held a three-game lead over slumping Seattle for a Wild Card spot. Only a crushing collapse could keep the team out of the playoffs.

Hosmer, Gordon, and Cain made sure that did not happen. Combining for nine hits and four RBI, the trio powered KC to a 6-3 victory over the Sox. The following night Jeremy Guthrie came through in a big way, tossing seven scoreless innings. When Salvador Perez caught the final out of the 3-1 triumph over Chicago, his teammates sprinted over to mob him near home plate. The victory secured a Wild Card spot for Kansas City. The longest active postseason drought in baseball—or any major North American sport—had finally ended. Joyful chaos reigned in the clubhouse as bubbly doused the playoff-bound Royals. "It feels better than expected," Billy Butler said. "It's a great thing." George Brett stood nearby, proudly surveying the boys who elevated the franchise to heights not seen since his own playing days.

But there was still unfinished business in the 2014 season. Kansas City led Oakland by just one game in the standings. They would need to maintain that lead to ensure the Wild Card Game would be played at Kauffman instead of the East Bay. And the Royals trailed Detroit by just one game in the AL Central. With two games left to go, a division crown still remained a possibility.

Opportunity beckoned the next day when Minnesota pounded Detroit 12-3. Danny Duffy unfortunately struggled with his command. The White Sox knocked him out early and staved off a late KC rally to win 5-4. Kansas City still trailed Detroit by one game, with one left to play. An Oakland loss to Texas, meanwhile, assured the Royals of the top Wild Card spot if they did not catch the Tigers.

Detroit's victory over Minnesota sucked the drama from Kansas City's final regular season contest. After learning that the division crown was out of reach, Yost pulled several starters from the lineup, including Yordano Ventura. The last game would have no impact on the Royals' postseason placement—the Wild Card Game was set for Tuesday night against Oakland at Kauffman Stadium. Yost wanted to ensure his team was well rested for the upcoming win-or-go-home contest. His boys nonetheless prevailed in the meaningless finale, 6-4.

Kansas City finished the season at 89-73. Joy, excitement, and optimism filled the clubhouse after that final game in Chicago. Players and coaches looked forward to sailing into uncharted postseason waters. "I'm glad we can kind of put the regular season behind us, [and] start this new journey right now," Hosmer said. "It's going to be a fun experience."

If he only knew.

Chapter 10

The Wild Card Game

Kansas City's Wild Card berth made news across the nation. Storylines abounded. A small-market team reaches the postseason while big spenders like the Yankees and Red Sox stay home. Perennial losers end a 29-year playoff drought. The weakling that always got sand kicked in his face finally stands up and fights back.

In the Midwest and beyond, Royals fans proudly wore attire emblazoned with the KC crown logo. Sports bars in the region swelled with blue-clad patrons. "We've been open ten years and we've never seen this kind of following for the Royals," said Dewayne Leer, owner of Uncle D's bar in St. Joseph, Missouri. The Kansas City bandwagon welcomed scores of new fans clamoring to celebrate the team's success. Indeed, for supporters of teams not in the playoffs, the underdog Royals became a popular "second" favorite team—Toronto fans perhaps serving as the exception. With Kansas City's Wild Card berth, the Blue Jays now owned the longest MLB postseason drought at 21 years.

For those Royals fans who remembered the glory days of George Brett and Frank White, the team's achievement was even more meaningful. Longsuffering fans woke up on Saturday, September 27th to a different reality. "It's a new-old feeling," said 41-year-old Ed Connealy, a writer for the Kings of Kauffman website. "It's pretty emotional because growing up as a little kid the Royals were a big part of my city's identity." Leer expressed similar sentiments. "It's hard ... to have them lose for so long and people talk bad about your team," the bar owner said. "... it just makes the victory that much sweeter to be where we are now."

Fan enthusiasm increased in anticipation of the upcoming postseason action. During the off day between the end of the season and the Wild Card Game, the Royals held a "Take the Crown" rally at Kauffman Stadium. Some die-hard parents even pulled their children out of school for the event. About 5,000 showed up at the rally, which included an opportunity to watch the players take batting practice. "I know people are excited, and you can see it on their faces, and I'm glad," Ned Yost said. "That's why home field advantage was so important to us, to bring this game back home for our fans."

Exciting as it was for what the Royals had already achieved, they still faced the prospect of their season ending in September. The Wild Card Game would be played on the month's final day, so losing would mean Kansas City again failed to play October baseball. For many fans of teams accustomed to postseason appearances, dropping the play-in game would be like not making the playoffs at all. While that was not true for Royals Nation, a one-and-done postseason would be a big letdown.

Regular season statistics generally favored Oakland heading into the one-game playoff. The A's scored 729 runs in 2014, third best in the American League; Kansas City scored just 651. Oakland batters drew 586 walks, tops in the AL; the Royals finished last in the league with 380 bases on balls. The A's slugged 146 home runs; Kansas City hit just 95 long balls—dead last in all the majors. Even more troubling, Oakland pitchers posted a 3.22 ERA, compared to 3.51 for KC hurlers.

On the other hand, the Royals batted .263 for the season, second best in the American League; Oakland batters hit .244.

Kansas City led the majors with 153 stolen bases; the A's managed just 83 thefts. The Royals tied for the AL lead with 53 saves; Oakland tied for last place with 31 saves. And Kansas City had the better gloves, ranking second in the AL in defensive runs saved.

A comparison of the starting pitchers tipped the odds back in favor of the A's. Throwing for two teams, Jon Lester finished the season with a 16-11 record and a 2.46 ERA—superior numbers to James Shields's 14-8, 3.21 ERA. Lester, moreover, boasted a career postseason ERA of 2.11 in eleven starts. That gave him the third best postseason ERA of *any* pitcher with at least ten such starts. In six postseason games, Shields had turned in a pedestrian 4.98 ERA.

The Royals nonetheless had reasons for optimism. The Boys in Blue had defeated Oakland five times in seven games during the regular season. And the factor of momentum could not be ignored. Kansas City had marched into the postseason with a 34-21 record over the last two months. The high of finally kicking down the door to the playoffs energized players and fans alike. Oakland, in contrast, limped into the postseason with a 22-33 record in August and September. During that span, the A's dropped from first place in the AL West to facing a must-win in their final game just to hang onto the second Wild Card spot.

Of course, momentum can change with a single pitch.

A LONG TIME COMING

Ten major league baseball teams qualified for the playoffs in 2014 (three division winners and two wild card teams per league). Of the ten teams, oddsmakers gave the Royals the worst chances (16 to 1) to win the World Series. The Angels and the Dodgers had the best odds at 5 to 1 each. For the American League pennant, Kansas City again had the worst odds at 7 to 1. Part of this lack of respect stemmed from the extra game the Royals had to play. All six division champs received a bye in the first round, leaving the wild card games to whittle the field down to eight. For fans and pundits across the nation, KC making the playoffs was a nice story. But few outside the Midwest believed the team could contend with the league powers.

Such opinions did not matter to the thousands of blue-clad fans filing into Kauffman Stadium on Tuesday night, September 30th. This was the biggest baseball game in Kansas City in nearly three decades, and the crowd prepared to rock. The team selected two KC natives for the pregame festivities. Maggie Marx, a student at Shawnee Mission Northwest High, sang the national anthem. World War II veteran Marlin Kerby threw the ceremonial first pitch. A Technical Sergeant in the U.S. Army Air Corps, the much-decorated Kerby flew sixty bombing missions before getting shot down and marched 600 miles to a German POW camp.

The Royals return to the postseason began with James Shields firing a strike to A's leadoff hitter Coco Crisp. After running the count full, Crisp singled to left. Retiring the next two batters, Shields prepared to face Brandon Moss. The A's cleanup hitter had struggled mightily after Billy Beane traded his teammate Yoenis Cespedes to acquire Lester. Given that Moss had batted just .170 since the All-Star Break, Big Game James had a decent chance to escape the inning unscathed. Instead, Moss drilled an 0-1 change-up into the right field seats above the visitors bullpen to put Oakland ahead 2-0.

Undaunted, the Royals went to work in the bottom of the inning. Alcides Escobar led off with an infield single. Nori Aoki grounded into a fielder's choice. With two outs, Aoki stole second during a four-pitch walk to Eric Hosmer. Billy Butler then ripped a single to left, scoring Aoki. But when Butler wandered too far off first, Lester caught him in a rundown that ended with Hosmer thrown out at the plate. Inning over, but Kansas City had broken through with a run.

Both pitchers cruised through a scoreless second. Trouble brewed in the third when Shields gave up back-to-back one-out singles. That put two on for Brandon Moss, ready to do more damage. With tension in the ballpark escalating, the A's cleanup hitter punched a soft liner snared by Hosmer, who threw over to Escobar to double off the runner at second. Crisis averted.

Mike Moustakas led off the KC third with a single to left. Trailing by just a run, Ned Yost opted to play small ball. Escobar laid down a sacrifice bunt to advance Moose to second. An Aoki ground out sent the runner to third. But with two outs, the sacrifice fly was no longer an option. Not a problem—Lorenzo Cain lined a double to left that scored Moustakas. Hosmer followed with a bloop hit to drive in Cain. The Royals led 3-2. The beyond-capacity crowd of 40,500 shouted with delight. Things were looking up. If the team could hold the lead three more innings, the Three-Headed Monster would come in to shut the door.

Both teams went down in order in the fourth and the fifth. The Royals were just three outs away from being able to deploy a bullpen that was the envy of all baseball.

But then disaster struck in the sixth. In the wake of five A's crossing the plate, sportswriters started pondering headlines:

"Brandon Moss Powers Oakland to Wild Card Victory"
"Yost Blunders Again"
"Nightmare End to Royals Postseason Dreams"

When Kansas City prepared to bat in the eighth still trailing 7-3, Royals Nation faced the prospect of a sudden, crushing end to their exciting season. Once again, the Boys in Blue would be denied October baseball.

ABSOLUTELY EPIC

In the bottom of the eighth, Escobar stood on third with one out. The roar of the never-say-die fans in his ears, Cain stepped into the batter's box to face Lester. With the season on the line, the Royals centerfielder rocketed a grounder up the middle, scoring Escobar. Kansas City trailed 7-4. At least the Royals would enter the off-season knowing they put up a fight.

Hosmer batted next. With a 2-2 count on the first baseman, Cain took off. It was this type of move that drove sabermetric devotees crazy. Down by three with just five outs left in the season, why did Yost's team employ such high-risk, low-reward tactics? Cain slid in safely. Lester walked Hosmer on a pitch that missed low and away. With the tying run stepping to the plate in the form of Billy Butler, Oakland manager Bob Melvin summoned reliever Luke Gregerson and his intimidating 2.12 ERA.

The pitching change made sense. Butler had batted just .255 against right-handed pitchers during the season. And despite the increasing excitement in the stadium, the A's were still firmly in command. No reason for the visitors to worry ... until Butler lined a single into right center. Cain scored; Hosmer advanced to third. With the tying run now on first, Yost sent Terrance Gore to run for Butler.

As Alex Gordon batted, Gore stole second. Gregerson then bounced a pitch into the dirt that got away from catcher Derek Norris. Hosmer raced home; Gore advanced to third; the crowd went nuts. Kansas City, left for dead just moments ago, now had the tying run ninety feet away with one out. All they needed was a sacrifice fly.

Gordon drew a walk to place runners at the corners. Salvador Perez stepped into the batter's box with a chance to be the hero. The Oakland reliever struck him out on three pitches. On the third strike Gordon stole second. The next batter, Omar Infante, could tie the game or even put the Royals ahead with a single. The crowd roared in anticipation. Gregerson struck out Infante to end the inning.

Kansas City had nonetheless narrowed the gap to 7-6. It had been a huge inning that elevated the energy in the home dugout. "We are not losing this game," Royals players shouted to each other, "we are winning this game!" But they still trailed by a run with just three outs left in their season. Though shaken, the A's retained the upper hand.

Although it was not a save situation, Yost called on Greg Holland to pitch the ninth. Facing the prospect of no tomorrow, Kansas City could not afford to give up any more runs. It would be a tense inning for the closer. He walked Sam Fuld with one out. After Josh Donaldson flew out to Gordon, Brandon Moss stepped to the plate. The Oakland cleanup hitter had already delivered two home runs and five RBI on the night. Another hit and he would finish off the Royals once and for all. Perez failed to glove a high delivery from Holland, sending Fuld to second. With first base open, the closer put Moss on first with an intentional walk. Holland then walked Josh Reddick—not intentionally—to load the bases. Disaster loomed. Pitching coach Dave Eiland visited the mound to settle down his reliever. Holland escaped when Jed Lowrie flew out to right to end the inning.

To nail down the Oakland victory, Melvin summoned his closer Sean Doolittle. Though his stats did not match Holland's, the southpaw had turned in a fine season, saving 22 games in 26 chances for the A's. His 2.73 ERA loomed even more ominous in light of his 89 strikeouts in 62.2 innings.

With a tough lefty on the mound, Yost pulled Moustakas for Josh Willingham. The pinch hitter led off the ninth with a blooper that dropped in right for a single. Yost sent Jarrod Dyson to run for Willingham. Escobar laid down a sacrifice bunt to advance the runner to second. Nori Aoki stepped to the plate needing just a single to tie the game.

Dyson had other ideas. In perhaps the boldest baserunning move of the game, he took off for third on a 2-1 pitch. Had he failed, the Royals would have nobody on with two outs. Kansas City's season would surely have been over.

Dyson slid in safely. KC had a man on third with one out. A sacrifice fly was all they needed to tie the game. And that is exactly what Aoki delivered—a fly ball to the warning track that scored Dyson. *That's what speed do.*

After nine innings, the game was tied at seven. For one team, this was great news. A four-run rally in the last two innings brought them back from the dead. For the other team, this was a less welcome development. Victory had slipped from their grasp. But the game was far from over. As both teams prepared for battle in extra innings, fans across the Midwest watched or listened with nervous intensity. Even Kansas City's finest were riveted, as indicated by this KC Police Department Twitter post: "We really need everyone not to commit crimes and drive safely right now. We'd like to hear the Royals clinch."

With Moustakas out of the game, Yost sent little-used Jayson Nix to play third. Cain shifted to right field to replace Aoki, while Dyson took over in center. Kansas City also sent a new pitcher to the mound. The A's may have lost momentum, but they did have one big advantage at this point—the Three-Headed Monster was done for the night. The Royals season now rested in the hands of Brandon Finnegan, the young lefty who pitched for his college team just months earlier.

As cool as a ten-year veteran, the former Horned Frog sent Oakland down in order in the top of the tenth. Kansas City put the winning run on third with two outs in the bottom of the inning, but Perez grounded out to end the frame.

Finnegan surrendered a two-out single, but otherwise had little trouble dispatching the A's in the top of the eleventh. In their half, the Royals again placed the winning run on third with two outs. Nix stepped to the plate with a chance to be an unlikely hero. The utility man had made just nine plate appearances after Kansas City claimed him off waivers in late August. Oakland reliever Dan Otero struck him out looking.

Finnegan again returned to the mound for the twelfth. Though effective thus far, the reliever walked Josh Reddick—never an ideal way to start an inning. Borrowing a page from KC's small ball manual, Lowrie bunted to advance the runner to second. Yost summoned Jason Frasor. Though not as celebrated as his bullpen counterparts, the veteran reliever had put up a formidable 1.53 ERA since a mid-season trade brought him to the Royals. Melvin countered by sending switch-hitting Alberto Callaspo to pinch hit. The veteran infielder had played for four teams in nine big league campaigns. In 2009 he batted .300 as the Royals second baseman. Five years later, he threatened to break the hearts of the very fans who once cheered him.

The situation worsened when Frasor bounced a wild pitch to give Oakland the go-ahead run at third with only one out. Callaspo then deposited a single into left to drive home a dagger. Frasor rebounded to retire the next two batters, but the damage had been done. Oakland led 8-7 and needed only three outs to advance. The Royals had fought and clawed out of a deep hole to send the game into extra innings. But with Callaspo's RBI, elimination hovered over Kauffman Stadium like the sword of Damocles. Did the Boys in Blue have enough left for one more comeback?

Cain led off the bottom of the twelfth by grounding out. The Royals were down to their final two outs. Hosmer stepped to the plate. He had reached base four times in five plate appearances. In the biggest at-bat of his career thus far, Hosmer hammered a drive to left center. As the ball slammed high off the wall and bounded away from the outfielders, the enthusiastic first baseman motored into third. Kansas City was back in business.

That brought up the designated hitter spot—normally Billy Butler. But Country Breakfast had been lifted for a pinch runner in the eighth. Yost tabbed rookie Christian Colon to fill the spot in the lineup. Though the 25-year-old only had 45 big league at-bats, he hit .333 in his limited opportunities. Otero fired to the plate. Colon hit a high chopper to third. Donaldson charged in, but could not make the barehanded grab. Hosmer raced home to again tie the game. Colon crossed first without a throw. Like a pendulum, momentum swung back to the home team.

Fernando Abad, a tough lefty specialist with a 1.57 ERA, came in to face Gordon. He threw one pitch, getting the KC slugger to pop out. With Perez up next, Melvin lifted Abad in favor of right-handed starter Jason Hammel. A ten-game winner with a 3.47 ERA, Hammel had limited righty batters to a .233 average on the year.

Colon stole second on a 1-2 pitch. It was Kansas City's seventh theft of the night, tying the postseason record for a single game. The Royals now had the winning run in scoring position. But Perez was 0 for 5 with two strikeouts in the game. The thirteenth inning seemed a likely possibility.

Looking for a strikeout, Hammel threw a slider just off the outside corner. Perez reached out and pulled it down the line, barely beyond the glove of Oakland third baseman Josh Donaldson. As the ball rolled toward the left field corner, Colon raced around third to score easily. After 4 hours and 45 minutes, Kansas City had won the AL Wild Card Game 9-8. The crowd roared in jubilation as the players mobbed their hero catcher.

"That's the most incredible game I've ever been a part of," said Yost. "Our guys never quit." The euphoric players echoed his sentiments. "This will go down as the craziest game I've ever played," Hosmer said.

Since Major League Baseball expanded the playoff field to ten teams in 2012, this was just the fifth wild card game. It was certainly the most memorable thus far, and probably would be for decades to come. As James Shields put it, "It was absolutely epic. You don't write a story like that."

Or maybe you do. The Royals story would continue …

Chapter 11

American League Division Series

For the first time since 1985, the Kansas City Royals would be playing meaningful games in October. By this point, the first six words of that sentence had become a common refrain. Because pretty much everything this team accomplished after mid-September could be prefaced by the phrase, *For the first time since 1985*.

The AL Wild Card Game had been a titanic struggle that lasted nearly five hours. Some commentators called it the greatest playoff game in major league history. It was certainly in the top five. Thrilling for the fans, exhausting for the players. The Royals prevailed, but they had little time to celebrate their victory. Just two days later, the team would open the American League Division Series against the Los Angeles Angels. The players didn't mind. "Not a lot of sleep, but that's OK," said Alex Gordon. "We'll take the lack of sleep for moving on and coming to L.A."

Having escaped the Wild Card frying pan, the Royals now entered the fire of facing the team with the best record in the majors. In winning 98 games, LA's power-laden lineup scored more runs than any other team in the league. Kansas City's advance to the ALDS was a nice story, but now Cinderella had to face the big boys: Mike Trout (soon-to-be-named 2014 MVP),

Albert Pujols (three-time MVP), Josh Hamilton (MVP, 2010), and David Freese (World Series MVP, 2011).

Comparing payrolls further highlighted the advantage held by the squad from southern California. Angels player salaries topped $128 million, well above the $90.5 million paid to the Royals. Los Angeles had used its financial resources to acquire a lineup of thumpers that slammed 60 more home runs than Kansas City, while outslugging Yost's boys .406 to .376. Though the Royals hit for a slightly better average, the Angels drew 112 more walks. KC stole nearly twice as many bases, but would that even matter against the Halos' thunder?

On the other hand, Kansas City may have dodged a bullet. Detroit, which owned a 13-6 head-to-head record against KC, would face Baltimore in the other ALDS. Kansas City and Los Angeles, in contrast, had split their six regular season games, with each side taking two of three at home. Oddsmakers nonetheless favored the Angels to win the series. Aside from their lineup advantages, the Halos were managed by Mike Scioscia, who had already guided his team to one world championship and was widely considered the better skipper. Most experts agreed with CBS baseball writer Matt Snyder's assessment: "[The Angels] are the superior team and that matters more than some narrative about an underdog."

Maybe Kansas City could win one game in the best-of-five series … maybe.

ALDS GAME 1

The American League Division Series opened at Angel Stadium of Anaheim on October 2nd. With James Shields unavailable, Ned Yost gave the ball to Jason Vargas. The left-hander had posted a solid 11-10, 3.71 ERA during the season. But he knew the heavy artillery of Mike Trout and company would pose a difficult challenge. When asked about facing the likely AL MVP, Vargas replied, "… you're going to have to negotiate that whole lineup, and if you think about one hitter, your work is going to be cut out for you."

Scioscia countered with 18-game winner Jered Weaver. Since breaking into the majors with an 11-2 record in 2006, the tall right-hander had been one of the best hurlers in the AL. The Angels ace had finished in the top five in Cy Young voting in three of the past five years.

Coincidentally, Vargas and Weaver had been close friends since college. As teammates at Long Beach State, the pair nearly led their team to the College World Series in 2004. A decade later, the former Dirtbags planned a joint vacation with their families in the offseason. But first they would square off against each other in the playoffs.

Vargas seemed headed for early trouble when Angels leadoff hitter Kole Calhoun launched his first pitch to deep right. The crowd rose in anticipation. But centerfielder Lorenzo Cain leaped high at the wall to rob Calhoun of extra bases. In the second, Cain again bailed out his pitcher with a sliding catch of a sinking drive by Erick Aybar.

After tossing two scoreless innings, Weaver walked Mike Moustakas with two down in the third. Alcides Escobar followed with a double, plating Kansas City's first run. In the bottom of the frame, the Angels tied it back up when their ninth-place hitter, catcher Chris Iannetta, deposited a hanging change-up into the bullpen beyond the left field fence.

After both sides went down in order the next inning, Alex Gordon led off the fifth with a double that centerfielder Mike Trout lost in the lights. Gordon moved to third with an opportunistic advance on Salvador Perez's fly out to the warning track in left. Omar Infante put the Royals on top with another sac fly. Yost's boys thus continued their small ball tactics of advancing runners with sacrifices. While the Royals followed their MO, so too did the Angels. In the bottom of the fifth, David Freese blasted a dinger to left to again tie the game.

Vargas wandered into trouble in the bottom of the sixth after surrendering a single to Calhoun and a two-out walk to Pujols.

Angels clean-up hitter Howie Kendrick appeared to have delivered a big blow when his drive to deep right center eluded the leaping Cain. But Nori Aoki made a dramatic backhanded grab behind Cain on the warning track to end the inning and prevent two Halo runs from scoring.

Yost unchained his bullpen beast in the seventh. But after walking Freese, Kelvin Herrera had to leave the game with tightness in his forearm. With Brandon Finnegan on the mound, the Angels advanced their runner to third with a sacrifice and a ground out. Looking to keep the game tied, Yost summoned Wade Davis. Angel designated hitter C.J. Cron hit a deep drive to right that brought the crowd to its feet when Aoki appeared to have misplayed it. But once again, the KC right fielder made a thrilling catch to end the threat.

With Weaver's exit after the seventh, the game became a battle of the bullpens. Both sets of relievers were up to the task, posting zeroes in the eighth, ninth, and tenth innings—though the Angels put runners on base in all three frames. In the eleventh, Scioscia sent Fernando Salas to the mound. A valuable bullpen weapon for the Halos, the reliever had posted a 5-0 regular season record with a 3.38 ERA.

Moustakas led off for the Royals. The KC third baseman, who batted .212 with 15 home runs in the regular season, ripped a high fly ball to right. "I knew I hit it pretty good, but that fence out there is pretty tall," the California native said. The fence was not tall enough for Angels fans—Moose's blast landed in the first row of the elevated stands to give Kansas City a 3-2 lead. Greg Holland retired the side in order in the bottom of the eleventh to close out the victory.

While Holland's save was relatively uneventful, the past three days of his life had been a whirlwind. After the Royals Wild Card victory on Tuesday, he flew to North Carolina for the imminent delivery of his first child. After his wife Lacey gave birth to Nash Gregory Holland on Wednesday evening, the new papa headed back to the airport for a chartered flight 2,000 miles across the continent. Holland arrived in Los Angeles around

4:00 Thursday afternoon, but traffic delays prevented him from reaching the stadium for three more hours. The game was in the fifth inning by the time the closer gained access to the ballpark. Fortunately, Kansas City would not need him until the eleventh. Interestingly enough, this was not the first time a Royals pitcher experienced the joy of fatherhood in the midst of the postseason. In October 1985 pitcher Bret Saberhagen became a first-time father when his son Drew was born the night before he pitched Game 7 of the World Series. Two decades later, Drew Saberhagen played college baseball at Western Carolina University. One of his teammates at WCU was … wait for it … Greg Holland!

Despite logging just four hits, Kansas City had captured Game 1. KC pitchers held the Halos' MVP trio of Trout, Pujols, and Hamilton to a combined 0 for 13. "This is the type of game we play," Yost commented afterwards. "We don't score a bunch of runs … so we have a lot of confidence in our pitching." It also sparked confidence that Moose, just months after being sent to the minors, produced a game-winning hit in October.

ALDS GAME 2

Los Angeles had amassed a 52-29 mark at The Big A in 2014, the best home record in the majors. Kansas City was lucky to steal the first game, but the possibility of taking two in a row in the Halos home park seemed remote. Especially since Angels phenom Matt Shoemaker would be taking the mound. The bearded rookie had posted a 16-4 record with a 3.04 ERA. Scioscia credited the right-hander with saving the Angels season.

To oppose Shoemaker, Yost called upon his own star rookie, Yordano Ventura. The Dominican flamethrower ended the regular season with a 14-10 mark and a 3.20 ERA. The last time the 23-year-old took the mound, however, he gave up a crushing three-run homer in the Wild Card Game. Would this setback, just three days earlier, remain in his head?

Concerns about Ventura increased after he surrendered a leadoff single to Calhoun. Trout grounded into fielder's choice, replacing Calhoun at first. With Pujols at the plate, the Angels MVP candidate took off for second. Perez, who threw out 30% of potential base stealers during the regular season, gunned down the runner. Pujols grounded out to end the inning.

Hosmer led off the Royals second by ripping a double into the right field corner. After a Billy Butler pop out, Gordon laced a single up the middle. Hosmer raced around third to score, and the Royals had once again taken an early lead.

Both hurlers found their groove by the third inning and the game settled into a pitchers' duel. Kendrick led off the Angels fifth with a single to right center. Aybar followed with a hit, giving LA two on with nobody out. As David Freese, no stranger to postseason heroics, stepped to the plate, trouble was brewing for Ventura. The young right-hander escaped when Freese hit a grounder to second that Infante and Escobar turned into a double play. Hamilton's fly ball to right ended the inning.

After retiring the first two batters in the sixth, Ventura looked to be cruising. But he gave up a single to Calhoun and then walked Trout. Two on with two out. Though hitless in the series thus far, the ever dangerous Pujols stepped to the plate. This time he came through with a single to right that scored Calhoun. After six innings, the game was tied at one apiece.

With Herrera still unavailable, Yost left Ventura in to pitch the seventh. The rookie retired the Angels in order. Wade Davis came on to pitch the eighth. To improve his late-inning outfield defense, Yost moved Cain to right and sent Jarrod Dyson to play center. After Davis gave up a leadoff double to Cron, Scioscia sent in Collin Cowgill to pinch run. The next batter, Iannetta, lofted a fly to left center that Dyson caught while moving right. Cowgill tried to advance—if he made it the Angels would have the winning run at third with only one out. Dyson fired a one-hopper to Moustakas, who applied the tag to eliminate the threat. *That's what defense do.*

The Royals put two men on with two out in the ninth, but failed to score. Jason Frasor retired the Angels in order in the bottom of the frame. With the game still deadlocked 1-1, Kansas City would be playing its third consecutive extra-inning postseason game.

After a scoreless tenth, Cain beat out an infield single with one out in the eleventh. That brought Eric Hosmer to the plate to face Kevin Jepsen. The hard-throwing Angels reliever boasted a 2.63 regular season ERA, while striking out 75 batters in just 65 innings. Hosmer was 0 for 5 in his career against Jepsen. Until this at-bat, that is. The Royals first baseman ripped the first pitch he saw over the right field wall to drive another eleventh-inning dagger into the Angels. Perez later plated Gordon with an insurance run to put KC up 4-1. New papa Holland came in to collect his second save in as many nights.

After finishing last in home runs during the regular season, the Royals had used the long ball to win two straight against the winningest team in the majors. Like his teammates, the latest KC hero relished his team's David role. "It's fun to be the underdog," Hosmer said. "It's fun to realize and go out there and play and know you don't have anything to lose and just put it all on the line."

Defensive hero Jarrod Dyson looked forward to returning home to play in front of the frenzied Royals fans. "I tell you what, I'm just happy they're having fun, right along with us," the outfielder said. "We're here and they're in Kansas City, and we can't wait to get back to our home crowd."

Despite their 2-0 advantage, the Royals still faced a powerful team determined to strike back. Commenting after Game 2, Pujols issued a stark reminder: "This series is not over."

ALDS GAME 3

The ALDS heading back to Kansas City with one team poised for a sweep was a situation that would not have surprised most baseball experts. That it was the Royals holding the brooms was the unexpected part. Though they had won more games than any other team in the majors, the Angels now sat one loss away from the off-season. Scioscia placed his team's hopes in the hands of C.J. Wilson. A decent pitcher in 2014 (13-10, 4.51 ERA), the southpaw had been one of the top starters in the American League a few years earlier when he helped the Rangers reach two consecutive World Series. LA could take heart that their man on the mound had more than 50 innings of postseason experience. But there was a cloud to that silver lining—Wilson's postseason record was 1-5.

Hoping to finish off the Angels, Yost turned to Big Game James. Though he encountered some rough sailing in his Wild Card outing, Shields was still the ace of the staff. He had the mentality needed to close out a series. His teammates had kept the Halo bats relatively quiet to this point. But with their backs to the wall, were the Angels now due to break out the heavy artillery?

The answer to that question appeared to be *yes* when Trout launched a monstrous home run into the left field fountains in the first. Los Angeles held a lead for the first time in the series. It would not last. In the bottom of the inning, Aoki and Cain singled with one out. After Hosmer took a called third strike, Butler drew a walk to load the bases. Gordon stepped to the plate with a chance to do some damage. And that is exactly what he did, hammering a 2-2 slider off the wall in left center. Billy Butler, summoning his inner gazelle, scored all the way from first. After the bases-clearing double, Scioscia pulled Wilson.

The Angels bullpen fared no better. Aoki led off the bottom of the third with a walk. After Cain popped out, Hosmer launched a towering shot over the centerfield wall. Kansas City led 5-1. Fans at The K roared in delight—the improbable was becoming likely. Butler added to the fun when, after drawing a walk, he took off for second. The Los Angeles defenders froze, paralyzed with shock at the rare sight of Country Breakfast trying to steal. Minutes later, Butler slid in safely with his first stolen base since 2012.

Pujols opened the fourth inning with a solo blast off Shields to cut the lead to 5-2. For the burly first baseman this game represented a homecoming of sorts. His family had moved to the Kansas City area in 1996 when he was a teenager. He watched his first major league ballgame at Kauffman Stadium. Though Pujols racked up impressive power numbers at Fort Osage High School in Independence and KC's Maple Woods Community College, he did not impress Royals scouts. Every other team passed on him as well—concerns about clumsiness and a flawed swing hurt his stock. Finally the Cardinals selected Pujols in the 13th round of the 1999 draft. So what did all those doubting scouts miss? Prince Albert batted over .310, hit at least 32 home runs, and drove in 100+ runs in *each* of his first ten seasons in the majors. He won three MVPs and finished runner-up four other times. To remind KC fans of the local boy they missed out on, he destroyed Royals pitching at The K. Of course, he destroyed pitching at pretty much every stadium across the league.

If Pujols's dinger in the top of the fourth reignited Angels' hopes, the bottom of the inning doused them again. With one out, Moustakas found the seats in right with his second homer of the series. Later in the inning, Cain hit a sacrifice fly to drive in Escobar. Kansas City led 7-2 and, with Herrera cleared to return, had a Three-Headed Monster poised to devour any chance of a Halo comeback.

Aided by a couple highlight reel diving grabs from Cain, Big Game James rolled through six strong innings. In the bottom of the sixth, Aoki plated Infante with another insurance run. For the top of the seventh, Yost removed Shields to start the lethal injection of H-D-H. Davis allowed a meaningless run in the eighth, otherwise the relievers had little trouble keeping the Angels at bay. Holland struck out Trout to finish off the 8-3 victory and an unlikely sweep. For the first time since 1985, Kansas City advanced to the American League Championship Series.

As the champagne flowed, reporters queried the conquering blue heroes on how they had made it to this point. Stolen base threat Billy Butler pointed to the balanced roster that Moore had assembled. "We have a ton of homegrown talent and mixed it in with a tremendous free-agent group and through trades," Country Breakfast said. Hosmer, who had belted two-run homers in each of the past two games, credited Gordon and his game-changing 3-RBI double. "That's a big reason he's the leader of our team," the first baseman said. "He really shifted the momentum there and got us feeling good."

Gordon in turn recognized that the Royals were now a battle-tested unit that generated a different clutch performer each night. "It doesn't matter who does it as long as somebody does it," the Gold Glove outfielder said. As for Yost, he saw a team that believed in themselves. "I've never seen this group of kids so confident on the big stage," the skipper said.

Yost's boys were indeed confident and ebullient after sweeping the team with the best record in baseball. Hosmer posted a Tweet inviting Royals fans to join the players for a celebration at McFadden's, a bar in downtown Kansas City. Arriving around 1:00 a.m., Hos and his teammates signed autographs, posed for pictures, and popped open a bottle or two. To further show his gratitude to KC's longsuffering fans, the first baseman pulled out his credit card and paid for an hour-long open bar for all the patrons at McFadden's.

The Royals had come a long way. But to achieve their goal of "Taking the Crown," they still had big hurdles to clear.

Chapter 12

A.L. Championship Series

Kansas Citians were not the only fans celebrating a postseason sweep on October 5th. Earlier that day, the Baltimore Orioles finished off the Detroit Tigers in the other ALDS. This was not unwelcome news in Royals Nation. The Boys in Blue would avoid facing their regular season nemesis and its Cy Young arsenal. Instead Kansas City would play Baltimore, a team it had defeated four times in seven games in 2014. And that is what the upcoming American League Championship Series would be—best four out of seven.

On the other hand, Baltimore's triumph may have been another "out of the frying pan into the fire" development for the Royals. Though unheralded at the start of the season, the Orioles got hot in the second half and raced ahead to win the American League East by a wide margin. Only the Angels had won more games than 96-66 Baltimore. The O's might have even compiled the best record in the majors had they not taken their foot off the pedal after clinching the division so early.

So who were these Orioles? As with the Royals, few experts predicted in the spring they would be one of the last four teams alive in October. And like Kansas City, Baltimore was playing in its first ALCS in the 21st century. But that is where the similarities ended—the two teams utilized vastly different approaches to win ballgames.

Baltimore slammed 211 home runs, best in all the majors. No other big league team topped 200. Kansas City, as mentioned earlier, finished last in the majors with 95 homers. Not surprisingly, the Orioles outslugged KC by a .422 to .376 margin, and bested them .734 to .690 in OPS. On the other hand, Baltimore recorded just 44 steals, less than a third of Kansas City's total. Of course, with that much power, why run?

The two teams were relatively even in pitching. Baltimore had a slightly better team ERA and could deploy four starters with ERAs of 3.65 or lower. Oriole relievers, though not as feared as KC's bullpen monster, got the job done as well. Zach Britton saved 37 games for the O's, while posting a sterling 1.65 ERA. Setup men Darren O'Day (1.70 ERA) and Tommy Hunter (2.97 ERA) headed an impressive supporting cast of relievers.

Baltimore would have been even more formidable had the team not lost three key players. Third baseman Manny Machado and catcher Matt Wieters, both Gold Glove winners and All-Stars, went down with season-ending injuries. Slugging first baseman Chris Davis and his 26 regular season home runs would also sit out the series after testing positive for amphetamines in September.

As for the men who would be calling the shots, Baltimore's Buck Showalter was one of the most respected managers in baseball. The Orioles skipper had won AL Manager of the Year three times—each with a different franchise. And this would be the fourth time he led a team in the postseason. Ned Yost, in contrast, was managing a playoff team for the first time. And his resume thus far had not impressed baseball pundits. Grantland's Ben Lindbergh wrote, "Yost has led a charmed life this postseason, as his bullpen decisions have either worked out or ultimately not mattered." Not surprisingly, most experts believed Baltimore held a big advantage in the manager category.

As small-market underdogs, Kansas City had become sentimental favorites across the country. An ESPN SportsNation poll revealed that 47 of the 50 states would be rooting for the Royals in the ALCS. The people who make their living predicting sports outcomes saw things differently. Though oddsmakers had grudgingly afforded some respect to the Royals, they still gave a clear edge to Baltimore. Betting odds forecast the O's as 2/3 favorites to win the series. Lindbergh expressed a common view when he predicted, "This isn't a lopsided series, but the odds are better than even that the Royals' running ends here. Orioles in six."

ALCS GAME 1

With five days off, both teams were well rested for the series opener at Camden Yards in Baltimore. James Shields would get the start for the visitors. The Kansas City ace had beaten the Orioles twice during the season and held an 11-7 lifetime record against Baltimore. Showalter gave the ball to Chris Tillman. The O's right-hander had turned in a laudable year, posting Shields-like numbers: 13-6, 3.34 ERA.

With neither team having played in a World Series since the 1980s, excitement surged through both fan bases. Anticipation spread among the players as well. "Both ballclubs are ready," Eric Hosmer said, "both ballclubs know the strength of their team and both ballclubs have done a good job of sticking to those strengths."

Baltimore threatened to draw first blood by loading the bases with two outs in the bottom of the second. The O's number nine hitter Jonathan Schoop stepped to the plate. He had batted just .209 during the season, but hit 16 home runs. A deep blast here might set the tone for the entire series. Shields escaped when Schoop popped out to Infante to end the inning.

Kansas City broke through in the top of the third when Alcides Escobar launched a high fastball over the left field wall. An unlikely power source, the shortstop had hit just three home runs during the year. Not content with just one run, the Royals loaded the bases with an Aoki single, a walk to Cain, and an infield hit by Butler. Batting with two outs, Alex Gordon lofted a broken-bat fly that landed fair just inside the right field line.

After Butler came around to score all the way from first, Gordon had his second bases-clearing double of the playoffs. Kansas City led 4-0.

Baltimore got on the board in the bottom of the inning when Adam Jones singled home Nick Markakis. The Royals soon pushed the lead back to four. Cain led off the top of the fifth by racing around first to stretch a single into a double. After he advanced to third on a Hosmer ground out, Butler drove him home with a sacrifice fly off reliever Tommy Hunter. It was textbook Royals baseball—the team would hit more sacrifice flies in the postseason than every other playoff team combined.

Shields sailed into the fifth with a 5-1 lead. But the waters grew choppy when he gave up back-to-back singles. After a fielder's choice ground out, Orioles DH Nelson Cruz stepped into the batter's box. Cruz had led the majors with 40 home runs. Though he did not homer this time, his drive off the left field wall scored a run and put O's at second and third. After a walk and a strikeout, Baltimore third baseman Ryan Flaherty lined a single that plated two more runs. The outburst left Kansas City clinging to a 5-4 lead.

With his starter reeling, Yost sent Brandon Finnegan to pitch the bottom of the sixth. The rookie southpaw immediately stepped in a mess by surrendering a walk and a single. During the next at-bat, Salvador Perez fired to second to catch Schoop wandering off the base. A golden opportunity to bag a much-needed out slipped away when Escobar's throw to Moose hit the runner, putting O's at second and third. A bloop from left fielder Alejandro De Aza dropped for an infield hit to tie the game. With runners at first and second and still nobody out, Yost brought in Kelvin Herrera. Adam Jones hit into a fielder's choice to erase the lead runner, but Moustakas's throwing error placed Orioles at the corners with just one out and the dangerous Cruz at the plate. Herrera got out of the jam with a potentially game-saving 6-4-3 double play.

Both bullpens kept the game knotted 5-5 heading into the ninth. Showalter called upon his closer Zach Britton to shut down KC in the top of the inning. The southpaw reliever instead walked the bases loaded with nobody out. Hosmer batted with a great chance to drive in the go-ahead run. But he grounded a two-hopper to first that Steve Pearce fielded and threw home to Nick Hundley to erase the lead runner. Not a great result, but the Royals still had the bases loaded with just one out. Showalter summoned right-hander Darren O'Day to face Billy Butler. Country Breakfast grounded into a double play and Kansas City squandered a huge opportunity.

Following this momentum boost, Baltimore batted in the bottom of the ninth needing just a single run to take Game 1. Wade Davis thought otherwise, striking out the side. For the fourth time in five postseason games, Kansas City headed to extra innings.

Showalter stuck with O'Day in the tenth. Gordon led off— just two innings earlier he had been hit in the neck by a 94-mph fastball. No problem. Much like Moose and Hosmer had done against the Angels, the left fielder blasted a home run to put KC ahead in extra innings. The dinger capped off a three-hit, four-RBI night for Gordon (plus a diving catch that saved a run), an outing that reminded many Royals fans of George Brett's Game 3 explosion in the 1985 ALCS. Moustakas added a two-run homer later in the inning to push the lead to 8-5. The team that had finished last in the majors in long balls continued to ride a power surge through the playoffs.

Baltimore scored once and put the winning run at the plate in the bottom of the tenth, before Holland squelched the rally to pick up the save. With the victory, Kansas City became the first team to win four extra-inning games in a single postseason.

Afterwards, Yost praised his slugging left fielder for shaking off a beanball that could have knocked him from the game. "Gordy just has a lot of confidence in his abilities," the manager said. "He's a guy that can [get] hit by a pitch and do exactly what he did, drive it out of the ballpark tonight...." Kansas City had now homered in four straight playoff games. "We didn't do it during the regular season," Gordon said about the unexpected power production. "But it doesn't really matter. This is the postseason, and we're starting to swing the bats better now."

ALCS GAME 2

The Royals had once again defeated a favored opponent on the road in the first game of a playoff series. If they could somehow win the second game, Baltimore would fall into a deep pit. Since Major League Baseball switched its league championship series to a best-of-seven format in 1985, no team had ever lost two LCS games at home and then come back to win. But how likely was another Kansas City victory? Baltimore boasted a 50-31 record at Camden Yards, the second best home record in the American League. And 15-game winner Bud Norris was starting for the O's. In addition to his strong regular season, Norris had shut down the Tigers with 6.1 scoreless innings in the final game of the ALDS.

Yost handed the ball to Yordano Ventura. Questions abounded among baseball analysts. Could a rookie keep the powerful Orioles bats in check? Could the Royals keep blasting clutch dingers in the late innings? Could Kansas City bury its well-managed opponents in an 0-2 hole?

The Royals wasted little time taking it to the O's again. With one out in the first, Aoki grounded a single into left. Cain followed by slashing a double into the right field corner to put men at second and third. Cleanup hitter Hosmer blooped a hit just beyond the glove of shortstop J.J. Hardy to plate both runners. Kansas City led 2-0.

Baltimore broke through against Ventura in the bottom of the second. The rookie opened the door for the home team by walking the bases loaded with one out. A sacrifice fly from catcher Caleb Joseph cut the KC lead in half. Ventura retired Schoop to escape with no further damage.

With two down in the top of the third, Cain beat out an infield chopper. After Hosmer lined a single to left, Butler drilled a double into the right field corner to extend the Royals lead to 3-1. Baltimore answered with its own two-out rally in the bottom of the inning. After a De Aza double, power-hitting Adam Jones blasted a Ventura fastball into the left field seats to tie the game.

The see-saw affair continued in the top of the fourth. Batting with two outs, Moustakas cleared the fence in right to put the Royals up 4-3. It was the fourth tater of the playoffs for Moose, who tied Willie Aikens for the most home runs by a Royal in a single postseason. A nice turnaround after the third baseman had hit just one long ball in his final 163 at-bats of the regular season.

Ventura preserved his team's slim lead until the fifth when De Aza and Jones touched him for back-to-back one-out singles. Cruz then grounded into a force out to plate De Aza. After five innings the game was tied at four apiece.

Ventura retired the first two batters he faced in the sixth before shoulder tightness forced him from the mound. After Finnegan got the third out, Yost predictably gave the ball to Herrera in the seventh. Baltimore loaded the bases with one out against the fireballing reliever, but failed to push across a run. Kansas City, however, could not score either. After Davis sent down the O's in the eighth, the contest headed to the ninth still tied 4-4.

Despite Darren O'Day's rough outing the previous evening, Showalter again trusted the reliever with the game on the line. Infante led off by beating out an infield dribbler. Yost sent in Terrance Gore to pinch run. Showalter summoned lefty Zach Britton to face Moustakas. Though Moose had been launching October homers like Reggie Jackson, his manager called for a sacrifice bunt. Moustakas laid it down, advancing Gore to second. That brought Escobar to the plate. For the second straight game the shortstop delivered a big hit, slapping a double down the right field line that scored Gore. After Jarrod Dyson reached on an error, Cain singled into left to drive home an insurance run.

Though not in extra innings, yet another late offensive outburst broke open a tie game for the Royals. Holland came in to preserve the 6-4 lead. Aside from allowing a single to Cruz, the Royals closer had little trouble slamming the door shut.

Similar to Gordon a day earlier, Cain had turned in a dominant performance with four hits (matching Brett's single-game postseason record), two runs scored, and an RBI. Cain also contributed a stolen base and an amazing diving catch in the outfield. His stellar outing continued what had been a memorable week for him. Like his teammate Greg Holland, Cain had just become a new father. Four days earlier his wife Jenny gave birth to their first child, Cameron Loe. The day after clinching against the Angels, Cain drove 370 miles from Kansas City to Norman, Oklahoma, to be with Jenny for the delivery. He then flew to Baltimore to join the team a day before the opening game of the ALCS.

Excitement abounded throughout the visitor's clubhouse after Game 2. "To come in here and win two games against a great team like that, it's huge for us," Moustakas said. His manager agreed. "If you could go home 1-1, you're going to be really, really happy," Yost said. "If you can go home 2-0, that's as good as it gets."

Both ball clubs were well aware that no team had won the first two games of a league championship series on the road and failed to win the series. "We don't want to be the first team to do that," Butler said. "That's all I get from that." In the other clubhouse, Oriole players remained confident that they could buck history. "If one team can do it, it's us," said Cruz. Echoing Albert Pujols from the ALDS, Adam Jones assured reporters, "This series ain't over."

ALCS GAME 3

The teams flew to Kansas City to play Game 3 on Monday evening, October 13th. Steady rain throughout the day, however, inundated the field. With the storm expected to continue through the night, Major League Baseball officials postponed the game until the following evening. Whether the delay would help the reeling Orioles or surging Royals remained to be seen. For their part, the players on both sides wanted to resume the action. "We're just really anxious to get back out there and play," Oriole Steve Pearce said. His first base counterpart on the Royals expressed similar feelings. "Whenever a team is hot, you definitely don't want rainouts or off-days," Hosmer said. "It's just Mother Nature. It's all part of life."

Jarrod Dyson, meanwhile, continued to entertain reporters with his confidence and candor. After raising eyebrows with an earlier comment about the series not returning to Baltimore, the speedy outfielder added more bulletin board material: "If we take Game 3, I guarantee there are going to be multiple people in that clubhouse over there saying, 'Man, there's no way we're going to beat these guys four games in a row.'" When asked to respond, the Orioles had little to say about Dyson's comments. "It doesn't matter what people think outside these doors," Nelson Cruz said. "That's my only answer."

Despite the extra day of rest, both managers decided to stick with their scheduled starters for Game 3. For Baltimore, Wei-Yin Chen would take the hill. The southpaw led his team in wins with a strong (16-6, 3.54 ERA) campaign in 2014. Yost countered with former Oriole Jeremy Guthrie (13-11, 4.13 ERA). Having not toed the rubber for 18 days, the KC right-hander would be making his first appearance in the postseason. Time would tell how the long layoff would affect the 35-year-old.

After a scoreless first inning, Pearce got the Orioles started with a one-out double off the left field wall in the second. Hardy then blasted a Guthrie fastball into deep right center for another double to drive in Pearce. Baltimore held a lead for the first time in the series. Guthrie walked the next batter, but escaped further damage with a fly out and a foul out. The veteran right-hander benefited from several nice fielding plays in the early innings, including a diving grab by Moustakas to rob Pearce of a hit in the fourth.

Chen, meanwhile, cruised through the first three innings. But with one out in the fourth, a jam-shot off the bat of Cain dropped in for a single. Hosmer followed with another blooper that fell for a hit. Billy Butler drew a walk to load the bases. Gordon stepped to the plate with a chance for his third bases-clearing double of the postseason. Though he did not do that, the bearded slugger drove home a key run with a ground out to second. The game headed to the fifth tied at one apiece.

Yost replaced Guthrie with Jason Frasor in the sixth. The new pitcher benefitted from more dazzling Royals glove work. Tracking an Adam Jones pop foul, Moustakas toppled into the third base dugout suite. KC fans caught the infielder, who held onto the ball. The play fired up the 40,000-plus spectators, who responded by roaring, "Mooooose." Aoki led off the Kansas City half of the inning with a single. Looking for the go-ahead run, Yost sent in Dyson to pinch run. After Cain struck out, Hosmer grounded a single into right that advanced the runner to third with just one out. Showalter brought in hard-throwing Kevin Gausman for a righty-righty matchup against Butler. Country Breakfast lifted a fly to left that easily scored the speedy Dyson. *That's what sac flies do.*

With a 2-1 lead, Yost unleashed the Three-Headed Monster for the final three innings. Herrera racked up two strikeouts while retiring the side in order in the seventh. Davis followed with a three-up, three-down eighth. Holland mowed down three more Orioles in the ninth to pick up the save. Counting Frasor's one-two-three sixth, Royals relievers retired all twelve men they faced. An especially critical accomplishment given that Kansas City was ahead by just one run.

And so the Royals' historic drive through the playoffs continued with another narrow victory. "We've got a snowball effect going right now," Butler said. "The confidence couldn't be any higher." With a commanding 3-0 advantage, Kansas City had its foot pressed on the Oriole necks. Of the 34 major league teams that had led 3-0 in a best-of-seven postseason series, only one—the 2004 New York Yankees—failed to win that series.

Despite having history on their side, the Boys in Blue knew they still had work to do. "We've got to zone in on the task at hand," said Holland. "They're not going to lay down." Indeed, the Orioles would not. "It's been done before, so that gives you a chance," said Adam Jones. "We've won four games before."

ALCS GAME 4

Because of Monday's rainout, Yost had the option of sending James Shields to the mound for Game 4 with his usual four-days rest. The KC skipper instead opted to stick with his original plan of starting Jason Vargas and leaving Shields ready for Game 5, if necessary. Needing to win four straight, Showalter similarly followed his plan of starting Miguel Gonzalez. The right-hander logged an impressive 3.23 ERA during the regular season, but had not pitched in 17 days. He would need to shake off the rust to have any chance of stopping the big blue steamroller.

With the pennant so close they could taste it, the Royals jumped on Gonzalez early. Escobar beat out an infield chopper to lead off the KC first. Gonzalez plunked Aoki in the leg to put men at first and second. Executing a typical Yost tactic, Cain laid down a sacrifice bunt to advance the runners to second and third. In so doing, Cain became the first number three hitter to drop a sac bunt in the postseason since Steve Garvey in the 1984 World Series. With an RBI opportunity, Hosmer hit a bouncer to the right side. Pearce fielded the ball and fired home, where Caleb Joseph put down the tag in time to get the runner. But Escobar's foot knocked the ball out of the catcher's mitt. Escobar was safe and Aoki raced around third to score while Joseph chased down the ball. Kansas City led 2-0.

After a quiet second inning, Orioles third baseman Ryan Flaherty led off the third by crushing a Vargas fastball deep down the right field line. The titanic blast stayed fair, landing high in the seats more than 430 feet from home plate. Baltimore had cut the lead in half, and it appeared this contest might become a high-scoring affair like Game 1.

Instead, both pitchers buckled down and the score remained 2-1 entering the fifth. In the top half of that inning Gordon made a spectacular catch, slamming hard into the left field fence to keep the O's from starting a rally. In the bottom of the inning, Aoki reached third with two outs. After intentionally walking Hosmer, Gonzalez ended the threat by inducing a ground out from Butler.

Vargas walked Baltimore's number nine hitter to start the sixth. The lefty then bounced back to strike out Nick Markakis. With the righty slugger Pearce batting next, Yost started the H-D-H treatment early. Herrera retired Pearce on a pop out, but then surrendered a single to Jones. With two on and two out, the dangerous Cruz stepped into the batter's box. He hit the ball hard, but Infante gloved the liner to end the threat.

Despite putting two men on with one out, Kansas City came up empty in the bottom of the sixth. Herrera retired the side in order in the seventh. Davis allowed a single in the eighth, but similarly emerged unscathed. The Royals were three outs away from the pennant.

Holland, as usual, came in to pitch the ninth. The capacity crowd stood and cheered—they would remain on their feet the entire inning. The reliever issued a leadoff walk to Jones. Baltimore had the tying run on base with Nelson Cruz, the major league home run leader, stepping to the plate. Tensions increased. In becoming one of the top closers in baseball, Holland had learned the best way to handle these situations: "Being able to take a deep breath, step off the mound, slow the game down and focus on what you need to do." Locked in on the task at hand, Holland got Cruz to tap a one-hopper back to the mound. The closer fielded the ball and threw to Escobar to force Jones at second. Delmon Young, a .300 hitter during the regular season, batted next. Holland struck him out. Shortstop J.J. Hardy represented the Orioles' last chance. Swinging at a 1-2 pitch, he grounded down the third base line. Moustakas backhanded it and threw over to Hosmer for the third out. In the words of broadcaster Denny Matthews: "Royals win it! ... Kansas City, you've got a World Series."

Fireworks exploded above the stadium. Players raced out to form a bouncing mass on the infield. Fans high-fived and yelled. George Brett cheered from his box. For just the third time in franchise history, the Kansas City Royals had won the American League pennant.

In the victors' clubhouse, champagne-drenched players celebrated and tried to explain how this team of underdogs had done it. "We're clicking at the right moment right now," said new papa Cain, who won the ALCS MVP after batting .533 in the four games. His manager added more specifics. "Athletic players, speed, defense, the ability to manufacture runs, not relying on home runs, and really good pitching," Yost said. Assistant GM J.J. Picollo elaborated on one of those factors. "They say hitting is contagious, but in this case I think the defense became contagious," the executive said. "It was just one guy outdoing the other."

The players expressed appreciation for their fans. "Running in from the outfield and seeing in the crowd and seeing all the energy after a lot of years of frustration," Gordon said, "it was pretty cool." For Holland, it was a dream come true to win the pennant at his home ballpark. "These fans have been waiting a long time," the closer said. "They deserve it." Moose concurred: "They've been waiting a lot longer than most of us have and it's an awesome feeling to be able to bring this American League championship to Kansas City."

In sweeping Baltimore, the Royals had won eight straight games to start a postseason. No team in baseball history had done that. And Ned Yost had won the first eight postseason games he had managed. No other big league skipper could make that claim. Not Joe Torre, not Tony La Russa, not Billy Martin, not Tommy Lasorda, not Casey Stengel or any of the other legendary managers of baseball past. None of them could match this accomplishment by the much-maligned Ned Yost. But the

KC manager rejected the idea that this pennant provided him validation. "I don't need validation, because I know who I am and I know what I'm about," he said. "I just wanted this for our fans, and I wanted it for our players."

Although October 15th was a day of celebration, talk inevitably shifted to the next challenge. Dayton Moore, the architect of this pennant-winner, summed up the prevailing clubhouse attitude about the upcoming World Series. "It's an unbelievable accomplishment to get where we are, and we want to enjoy this," the GM said. "But our guys will be ready to compete."

Dayton Moore, James Shields, Wade Davis, and Ned Yost after the December 2012 trade that brought the two pitchers to Kansas City. Though excoriated by analysts for giving up top prospect Wil Myers in this deal, Moore was vindicated when Shields and Davis played key roles in the Royals drive to the AL pennant. *Denny Medley-USA TODAY Sports*

Country Breakfast on the video board at The K.

Eric Hosmer hitting the decisive home run in Game 2 of the ALDS.
Kirby Lee-USA TODAY Sports

Second baseman Omar Infante watches shortstop Alcides Escobar turn a double play in Game 6 of the World Series. *Christopher Hanewinckel-USA TODAY Sports*

Catcher Salvador Perez visits Jason Vargas on the mound during a game against the Cardinals at Kauffman Stadium. *Denny Medley-USA TODAY Sports*

Third baseman Mike Moustakas congratulates Kelvin Herrera after the reliever retired the Angels in order in the seventh inning of Game 3 of the ALDS. *John Rieger-USA TODAY Sports*

Greg Holland jogging to the mound. The closer recorded 46 saves during the 2014 regular season and seven more during the postseason.

Outfielders Lorenzo Cain and Nori Aoki lunge for a deep fly during Game 1 of the ALDS. With the game tied in the sixth, Aoki made a dramatic catch to prevent two Angels base runners from scoring. *Kirby Lee-USA TODAY Sports*

Lorenzo Cain robs Baltimore shortstop J.J. Hardy of a hit during Game 2 of the ALCS – one of many highlight reel grabs the Royals centerfielder made during the postseason.
Tommy Gilligan-USA TODAY Sports

Yordano Ventura fires a pitch during Game 6 of the World Series. The rookie right-hander finished the regular season with a 14-10 record and a 3.20 ERA.
Pool photo-USA TODAY Sports

Billy Butler and Jarrod Dyson hoist the American League championship trophy after the pennant-clinching victory over the Orioles.
Denny Medley-USA TODAY Sports

Owner David Glass celebrates the Royals' league championship with Ned Yost and Dayton Moore. Though this trio received plenty of criticism over the years, they each made crucial decisions that helped bring the pennant to Kansas City in 2014.
Denny Medley-USA TODAY Sports

The fountains beyond the outfield wall remain one of the best-known features of Kauffman Stadium.

Greg Holland throws a pitch during the ninth inning of Game 7 of the World Series.
Peter G. Aiken-USA TODAY Sports

Alex Gordon bats with Eric Hosmer on third during Game 2 of the World Series.

Chapter 13

The World Series

Of the three Kansas City teams to reach the World Series, the Yost-led edition sent the greatest shock waves through the sports world. Yes, the 1980 and 1985 squads had to overcome formidable barriers, but their respective ascents did not cause a realignment of the baseball planets. The Brett-era pennants came during a ten-year span when the Royals were perennial contenders and postseason attendees. The 2014 team, in contrast, followed a much different path. Kansas City lost at least 90 games each season from 2009 to 2012. Only twice in the previous 19 seasons had the team finished above .500.

The blue resurgence thus became the top sports story of October 2014. Pundits across the nation weighed in on the development. "In baseball, something as preposterous sounding (on Opening Day) as 'World Champion Kansas City Royals' can actually happen," wrote Thomas Boswell for *The Washington Post*. "In what other hugely popular American sport is there an equivalent possibility?"

And it was not just that the Royals had made it to the World Series, it was how they got there—sweeping away three favored opponents. "Prior to this month, the focus was on how the Royals hadn't played a postseason game since 1985, the longest drought in baseball," ESPN's Jim Caple wrote. "Now they haven't lost a postseason game since 1985, the longest winning streak in baseball."

And KC looked to continue this streak. As ESPN's Jerry Crasnick wrote, "Don't dare tell the Kansas City Royals that it's been a noble effort and the 2014 season has been a raging success regardless of what happens from here." Indeed, having climbed this far, the Boys in Blue yearned to win it all. "These guys are hungry, man," Eric Hosmer said. "Everyone in here. We got no quit in us, and we believe we can do this."

One final hurdle remained—the San Francisco Giants. At first glance, it appeared the Royals may have caught a break. They did not have to face either of the two winningest teams in the National League—Washington or Los Angeles. Nor would they square off against their in-state rivals from St. Louis, who, remembering Denkinger, would have loved a shot at ending KC's magical run. Instead, Kansas City would face another wild card team.

Finishing the regular season at 88-74, San Francisco rode a similar wave through October as their blue counterparts. Hitting the road for the NL Wild Card Game, the Giants steamrolled Pittsburgh behind the shutout pitching of Madison Bumgarner. In the division round, San Francisco faced Washington, the team with the best record in the National League. With a balanced run-producing lineup and the lowest ERA in the NL, the Nationals would be tough to derail. Game 2 proved to be the key contest, which the Giants tied in the ninth and then won in the 18th inning. Though Washington rebounded from that grueling setback to beat Bumgarner two nights later, the Giants finished them off in four.

San Francisco battled St. Louis in the NLCS. Though the Cardinals did not appear as formidable on paper as the Nationals, they did boast a solid one-two pitching punch with Cy Young candidate Adam Wainwright (20-9, 2.38 ERA) and Lance Lynn (15-10, 2.74 ERA). More importantly, the Redbirds featured a sterling playoff pedigree, appearing in eight of eleven postseasons since 2004—including four pennants and two World

Series victories. Of course, as world champions in 2010 and 2012, the Giants knew plenty about how to win in October. Though the games were close, San Francisco prevailed in five— much to the disappointment of fans hoping for an I-70 Series rematch.

The Giants deployed an impressive offense that ranked fourth in the National League in batting average and runs scored. Their dangerous lineup included Pablo Sandoval (.279/.324/.415), Hunter Pence (.277/.332/.445), and former-MVP catcher Buster Posey (.311/.364/.490). On the pitching side, San Francisco's ERA of 3.50 fell in the middle of the NL pack. But the team did have a true ace in Madison Bumgarner (18-10, 2.98 ERA), who excelled in October. LA's Clayton Kershaw may have dominated the recent regular seasons with his annual ERA titles and Cy Young trophies, but Bumgarner was the hurler opposing teams dreaded most in the postseason. Cy Young winners Jake Peavy and Tim Lincecum, along with veterans Tim Hudson and Ryan Vogelsong, filled out the Giants starting rotation.

Experts had trouble picking a clear favorite in this World Series matchup of wild card teams. Both sides had momentum after knocking off league powerhouses. The Royals rolled in with a monster bullpen, stellar defense, team speed, timely hitting, and a fan-fueled mojo that defied explanation. The Giants countered with the best postseason starter in baseball, a balanced lineup, a decent bullpen, the managerial genius of Bruce Bochy, and World Series experience. Intangible factors favoring the Royals included their three-game sweep over the Giants in August and the wave of national sentiment supporting their unlikely run. The Giants, for their part, owned a $58 million advantage in payroll and a recent string of even-numbered year dominance.

Though oddsmakers gave Kansas City a slight edge to win, the Series was for the most part a toss-up. Perhaps the best pre-World Series forecast came from Jesse Spector of *Sporting News*, who predicted that the fans watching the games would be the true winners. "These are both fun teams who have earned their way here by playing excellent baseball," Spector wrote, "and if you're a fan of the game, it's hard not to have enjoyed this carnival ride of a playoff campaign."

WORLD SERIES GAME 1

Kansas City did hold one tangible edge that could potentially impact the games—home field advantage. Because of the American League's victory in the All-Star Game in July, Games 1 & 2 and Games 6 & 7 of the World Series would be played at Kauffman Stadium. Thank you, Mike Trout.

A festival atmosphere prevailed at The K in the late afternoon of October 21st. Longtime Royals groundskeeper George Toma, for decades the best in the business, came out of retirement to help prepare the field. Fans gathered early in the vast parking lot of the Harry S. Truman Sports Complex. As game time approached, the enthusiastic blue masses migrated toward the ballpark gates. Ushers greeted them by proclaiming, "Welcome to the World Series!" Inside the stadium, the capacity crowd included several celebrities pulling for the home team. Among these luminaries were Paul Rudd, Eric Stonestreet, Jeff Foxworthy, and superfan SungWoo Lee.

Country star Trisha Yearwood sang the national anthem. Honoring the nation's military personnel, the Royals selected U.S. Army Staff Sergeant Pedro Sotelo, decorated for his special operations service in Iraq, to throw out the ceremonial first pitch. Surrounded by a sea of towel-waving fans, Sotelo, clad in his dress uniform, tossed a strike to Jeremy Guthrie. Moments later, the Royals took the field.

A James Shields fastball to Giants leadoff hitter Gregor Blanco marked the first World Series pitch thrown in Kansas City since Bret Saberhagen's final delivery to Andy Van Slyke in Game 7 of the 1985 Series. The event Royals fans had waited nearly three decades to see was now a reality. But it did not take long for the party to sour for the blue revelers.

Blanco slapped a flare to center that dropped in front of Cain. After a sac fly advanced the runner, Buster Posey lined a single to left, putting runners at the corners. Third baseman Pablo Sandoval, the "Kung Fu Panda," drilled a low curve into the right field corner, scoring Blanco. Kansas City avoided further trouble when Aoki hit relay-man Infante, who gunned down Posey at the plate. With one on and two out, Shields had a chance to escape with minimal damage. Right fielder Hunter Pence had other ideas, mashing a two-run shot over the centerfield wall. San Francisco led 3-0.

Bumgarner, meanwhile, was as good as advertised. He breezed through the first two innings, retiring six of the first seven he faced. In the third, Kansas City landed a couple blows to back him into the ropes. Infante reached on an error by shortstop Brandon Crawford. Moustakas ripped a double into the right field corner to put men at second and third with nobody out. KC had a golden opportunity to get on the board. But then Bumgarner clamped down the way "MadBum" tends to do in October. He struck out Escobar. He struck out Aoki. After walking Cain, he ended the inning with a Hosmer ground out. The Royals would get nothing and like it.

Shields again wandered into trouble in the fourth. Pence led off the inning with a double. After a wild pitch and a walk to first baseman Brandon Belt, the Giants had runners at the corners. Unlike the home team, San Francisco would not waste the opportunity. Designated hitter Michael Morse looped a single to center, scoring Pence. The hit ended Shields's evening. Yost brought in Danny Duffy to stop the bleeding. The young lefty walked the next batter to load the bases, and then issued another walk to plate a run. San Francisco led 5-0.

It might as well have been 50-0. Retiring the Royals in order in the fourth, fifth, and sixth, Bumgarner rode a two-hit shutout into the seventh. Even more daunting, he had pitched 21 consecutive World Series innings without allowing a run—a streak that dated back to 2010. San Francisco scored two more in the top of the seventh to dash any faint hopes still held by the most die-hard of KC supporters.

Salvador Perez gave Royals fans something to cheer in the bottom of the seventh when he smacked a two-out homer to left. The blast ended Bumgarner's scoreless streak in the World Series, but had no impact on the outcome of the game. San Francisco's bullpen kept the Royals at bay in the final two innings to complete the 7-1 victory.

And so the long-awaited Kansas City World Series extravaganza began with a thud. Their postseason winning streak over, the team tasted defeat for the first time in more than three weeks. To make matters worse, Royals fans became the target of taunts from an unlikely source—TV and movie star Rob Lowe. It was bad enough that viewers watching the Series on Fox had to endure an endless repetition of "Creepy" Rob Lowe commercials for DirecTV. Now, the former *West Wing* star tweeted, "The big stage is the big stage. The spotlight ain't for everyone."

While Royals fans responded with a torrent of rebuttals, Lowe did raise a legitimate question. Had time run out for this season's Cinderella? There had been several instances in baseball past when an underdog team caught fire late to blaze into October. In 2007, for example, the Colorado Rockies won 14 of their last 15 games to reach the postseason for just the second time in franchise history. The team then won seven straight playoff games to sweep the NLDS and NLCS. But in the World Series they crashed to earth, losing 13-1 to Boston in Game 1. The Red Sox went on to sweep all four games. Were the Royals destined to be the Rockies of 2014?

WORLD SERIES GAME 2

On the plus side, the Royals would not have to worry about Madison Bumgarner in Game 2. But they would be facing a former Cy Young winner in the form of Jake Peavy. The veteran right-hander had pitched effectively (6-4, 2.17 ERA) since the

Giants acquired him from Boston in late July. And Peavy, unlike any other player on either roster, was playing in his second consecutive World Series, having helped the Red Sox bring home the title a year earlier.

While Bochy's starter bristled with experience, Yost countered with a rookie—Yordano Ventura. The Pedro Martinez protégé had pitched three times thus far in the postseason, surrendering seven runs in 13 innings. Game 2 was technically not a must-win for Kansas City—the 1985 team dropped its first two Series games at home—but losing this contest to the experienced Giants would plunge them into a Grand Canyon-sized hole. For all intents and purposes, the 2014 season now rested in the right hand of a 23-year-old making his first appearance on baseball's biggest stage.

The Royals selected George Brett to throw out the ceremonial first pitch. Seeing Number 5 on the field energized the crowd. Less pleasing to the fans was Gregor Blanco's leadoff home run into the right field bullpen. Just one batter into the game, the Giants had picked up where they left off in Game 1. Could that pretty man from *St. Elmo's Fire* have been right? Was the Series headed for a sweep?

Alcides Escobar began the Royals first with an infield hit off the glove of Brandon Crawford. After an Aoki fly out, the fleet shortstop tried to steal. It was no secret that Kansas City hoped to reignite its running game for the Series. Posey gunned him down. With two out and nobody on, Cain drove a hit into left center that he legged out for a double. Hosmer followed by drawing a walk. Billy Butler stepped to the plate. With the crowd standing in anticipation, the popular DH ripped a single past the shortstop to drive home the tying run.

An inning later, Omar Infante hammered a one-out double to left. After Moustakas flew out, it looked like Infante might be stranded at second. Escobar came to the rescue with his second hit of the night. This time he laced a double down the right field line to give the Royals their first lead of the series.

Both pitchers cruised through the third, and the game appeared to be settling into a pitchers' duel. Ventura needed to hold the lead for just three more innings before H-D-H time. Sandoval put this plan in jeopardy in the fourth by drilling a shot to the centerfield wall for a double. After a Pence ground out, Brandon Belt smoked another double into the right field corner. The game was knotted at two apiece.

With the game still tied, Yost deployed his outfield upgrade in the sixth—Jarrod Dyson went in to play center and Cain shifted to right. Posey led off the frame with a single. After the Panda flew out, Pence stepped to the plate. Throughout the ballpark, Royals fans raised signs ribbing the outfielder. This practice actually began the previous summer when the Giants played the Mets in New York. The trolling of Pence continued the rest of the season at other stadiums, including Kauffman, where fans held signs proclaiming that "Hunter Pence thinks he's in Kansas" and "Hunter Pence thinks burgers are barbeque." Not bothered by the extra attention, Pence reached base with an infield hit to put runners at first and second. Yost brought in Kelvin Herrera. The first head of the bullpen monster devoured the Giants rally with barely-visible 101-mph fastballs.

Lorenzo Cain led off the bottom of the sixth by dropping a single into center. After Peavy walked Hosmer, Bochy pulled his starter in favor of Jean Machi. Butler greeted the reliever with his second RBI-single of the night to score Cain. Bochy brought in lefty Javier Lopez, who retired Gordon on a fly out. Hard-throwing Hunter Strickland then came in to face Salvador Perez. The Royals catcher ripped a double into the left-centerfield gap to plate Hosmer and pinch-runner Terrance Gore. Infante followed by rocketing a two-run homer into the left field bullpen. As the runners rounded the bases, Strickland yelled into his glove in frustration. Crossing the plate, Perez thought the pitcher was shouting at him. More yelling ensued and the dugouts emptied. Umpires and coaches quickly restored order to prevent a brawl. Bochy replaced Strickland with Jeremy Affeldt, the fifth Giant to pitch in the inning. That had not happened in a

World Series since 1985 when five Cardinals pitched in the fifth inning of Game 7. After a Moustakas single, Escobar grounded into a double play to end the frame. Kansas City had scored five to take a 7-2 lead.

Herrera overcame two walks to pitch a scoreless seventh. Wade Davis struck out two while retiring the side in order in the eighth. Greg Holland gave up a single in the ninth, before striking out the next three batters. H-D-H had logged 3.2 scoreless innings to preserve the victory.

The Kansas City triumph changed the entire outlook of the Series. "We showed them that we have fight in us," Billy Butler said, perhaps referring to the score as well as the sixth-inning dustup. Giants manager Bruce Bochy agreed. "With their pitching and our pitching, and the way both teams play," the manager said, "we're going to have a fight, I think, every game." With the Series tied 1-1, the two teams would fly to San Francisco for the next three games. If either team swept those contests, Kauffman Stadium had seen its last baseball of 2014.

Somehow, that did not seem likely.

WORLD SERIES GAME 3

As the Series shifted to AT&T Park in San Francisco, Ned Yost faced a new challenge in setting his lineup. In the National League ballpark he could not use a designated hitter. Instead, per NL rules, the pitchers would bat. The Giants were used to playing this way, the Royals were not. Billy Butler would have to sit. Advantage home team.

Bochy chose Tim Hudson to start Game 3. The veteran right-hander had won 214 games over sixteen years in the majors. At age 39, he would be starting his first World Series game. Though not as dominant as in his early days with Oakland, Hudson posted a respectable 3.57 ERA over 31 starts in 2014.

Kansas City similarly started a long-tenured veteran— Jeremy Guthrie. Like Hudson, the 35-year-old would be making his first World Series start. Behind Guthrie, Yost made a defensive change. To better cover the peculiar outfield dimensions of AT&T Park, he started Dyson in center and Cain in right. Aoki would thus join Butler on the bench. And seeking more thump early in his lineup, Yost moved Gordon, who led the Royals with 19 regular season home runs and 74 RBI, from sixth to second in the batting order. Moustakas moved up from ninth to fifth.

Kansas City wasted no time attacking Hudson. Country quartet Little Big Town had barely finished the national anthem when Escobar hammered the right-hander's first pitch off the left field wall for a leadoff double. Gordon, similarly first-pitch swinging, grounded to first to advance the runner. Cain drove Escobar home with a grounder to shortstop Brandon Crawford, and the Royals grabbed the lead.

After KC's early fireworks, both starters settled into a groove. Kansas City's fielders once again supplied timely help for their man on the mound. Cain made two beautiful sliding catches to prevent sinking liners from dropping in for hits. In the second inning, Perez cut down Pence trying to steal. Belt followed the failed theft attempt with a single. After that hit, Guthrie retired the next ten Giants he faced. Not to be outdone, Hudson sent down twelve consecutive Royals. The veteran pitchers combined for a streak of retired batters not seen in the World Series since Don Larsen's perfect game in 1956.

The contest remained 1-0 heading into the sixth. With one out, Escobar singled up the middle. Gordon followed by clubbing an RBI double over Blanco's head in center. After Cain grounded out, Bochy tabbed Javier Lopez to relieve Hudson. Hosmer battled the left-hander through an 11-pitch at-bat that ended with a line drive up the middle to plate Gordon. Kansas City led 3-0. For Hosmer it was his first hit of the World Series—an appropriate way to celebrate his 25th birthday.

The Giants struck back in the bottom of the sixth. Crawford led off with a single. Pinch hitter Michael Morse scorched a double down the left field line to score Crawford. Yost decided it was time to release the beast. Herrera walked Blanco to put two men on with no outs. Second baseman Joe Panik chopped a high bouncer to the pitcher that advanced the runners to second and third. Posey followed with a grounder to Infante that scored Morse. Herrera retired Sandoval to end the inning, but San Francisco had cut the lead to 3-2.

After walking Pence to start the Giants seventh, Herrera rebounded to strike out Belt. With lefty-hitting Travis Ishikawa stepping to the plate, Yost brought in Brandon Finnegan. The 21-year-old southpaw became the first player ever to appear in the College World Series and Major League World Series in the same year. Bochy sent righty-batting Juan Perez to pinch hit for Ishikawa. Finnegan retired him on a fly out and then struck out Crawford to end the inning.

Wade Davis sent the Giants down in order in the eighth. Holland came on to pitch the ninth. Days earlier he revealed that as a kid he had dreamed of playing in the World Series—but not as a pitcher. "I was an infielder hitting the game-winning home run," Holland said. Now as an adult, it was his job to prevent the game-winning hit in a World Series. And he would have to face the dangerous triumvirate of Posey, Sandoval, and Pence with just a one-run lead. Holland retired them one-two-three. With yet another dominating performance from the bullpen, Kansas City led the Series two games to one.

It was a textbook Royals victory, complete with small ball runner advances, stellar defense, timely hits, and lockdown relief pitching. Yost of course still took criticism—this time for not pinch hitting for his pitchers in the sixth and seventh—but his moves continued to work. When asked about the possibility of his decisions backfiring, the skipper responded in typical Yost fashion: "I didn't lose the game, so I don't think about that stuff." The manager later explained how he was able to win so many one-run contests. "It's the guys that we put out there that are doing it," Yost said. "We have the type of pitchers in our bullpen that can accomplish that."

And now Yost and his guys were just two games away from a world championship.

WORLD SERIES GAME 4

With his team trailing in the Series, Bruce Bochy had a decision to make. Facing the prospect of falling into a 1-3 hole, Bochy could stick with his scheduled starter for Game 4, Ryan Vogelsong, or give the ball to his ace Bumgarner. Vogelsong's 2014 numbers (8-13, 4.00 ERA) did not inspire confidence. But MadBum would be pitching on short rest, not usually a recipe for success. Adding to the case for Plan A was Vogelsong's past postseason results: 3-0 with a 2.16 ERA in six starts. Plus, he was more effective at home. And finally, articulating what was likely the deciding factor, Bochy said, "If Madison pitched tomorrow [in Game 4], we're still going to have to pitch somebody the next day [in Game 5]."

So it would be Vogelsong for the Giants. Opposing him for the Royals was Jason Vargas. The veteran lefty had pitched well in two postseason starts thus far. With MadBum looming in Game 5, Vargas hoped to keep the momentum rolling for the big blue machine.

Vargas got off on the wrong foot when he walked Blanco to open the bottom of the first. The Giants centerfielder moved to second on a wild pitch and, following a Joe Panik pop out, stole third. Posey walked to put runners on the corners with just one down. The next batter, Pence, grounded sharply to third. Moustakas fielded it and threw to Infante, who fired to Hosmer to try to complete an inning-ending double play. But Pence, sprinting mightily, barely beat the throw to allow the run to score. The Giants led 1-0 without a hit.

In the top of the third, Gordon stood at first with two outs. Vogelsong had allowed three hits, but had kept the Royals from scoring. After Gordon stole second, Cain hit a slow bouncer to the left side that he beat out for an infield hit. With runners at the corners, Kansas City's speed had once again kindled a rally.

Hosmer chopped a dribbler to the right side that Belt fielded and tossed to Vogelsong covering first. But the pitcher could not find the bag in time. Hosmer was safe and Gordon scored the tying run. Bochy flung down his cap in disgust. Moustakas walked to load the bases. Infante followed by drilling a single up the middle to score Cain and Hosmer. Continuing the two-out uprising, Salvador Perez dropped a single into shallow center to plate Moose. Vogelsong's night was over. The Royals led 4-1.

With the Giants on the ropes, pinch hitter Matt Duffy led off the bottom of the third with a single. A ground out advanced him to second, where he remained with two outs and Posey stepping to the plate. The former MVP delivered a clutch hit to drive home the run. San Francisco had cut the lead to two.

The game remained 4-2 heading to the bottom of the fifth. In the Royals bullpen the growling monster rattled its cage, waiting for the gate to rise so it could rush forth and devour. Panik started the frame with a double to right center. That was it for Vargas. Yost brought in Jason Frasor to get a few key outs before the release of H-D-H. Posey grounded to Escobar, advancing the runner to third. So far so good. But then Pence slapped an RBI single to center, cutting the lead to one. Yost brought in lefty Danny Duffy to force switch-hitting Sandoval to bat from the right side. It made sense—the Panda had hit only .199 as a righty in the regular season. But he swatted a single to left center, sending Pence to third. Duffy walked Belt to load the bases with just one out. Juan Perez then lofted a fly to shallow center that was about to drop for another hit, before the charging Dyson made a great diving catch. Outstanding defense indeed, but Pence alertly tagged up on the play and raced home to tie the game at four.

Even though they had lost the lead, the Royals were still in a good position. The team had prevailed in several postseason games that were tied in the late innings. With their dominant bullpen and penchant for clutch hitting, things still looked good for the Boys in Blue.

Until the bottom of the sixth, that is. Brandon Finnegan came on to pitch. Two quick singles and a sacrifice bunt put runners at second and third with just one out. Finnegan intentionally walked Posey to load the bases. With the infield drawn in, Pence grounded to Escobar who threw home to stop the go-ahead run from scoring. The bases were still loaded, but now there were two outs. The young lefty had a chance to escape unscathed. Sandoval batted from the right side—just where the Royals wanted him. Until the Panda laced a single to center that plated two runs. With the orange and black crowd rocking, Belt followed with another RBI hit. The Giants led 7-4.

In the bottom of the seventh, San Francisco roughed up Finnegan and Tim Collins for four more runs. What looked to be a tight battle had turned into a rout. In the eighth inning, former Journey front man Steve Perry led San Francisco fans in singing the classic rock ballad "Lights." By that time, unfortunately, the lights had long since gone out on KC's chances in this game.

The 11-4 shellacking left the series tied at two games apiece. By scoring ten unanswered runs, the Giants had figured out how to beat the Three-Headed Monster—don't let it get into the game. "This was a great ballgame, I thought," Bochy said, "especially the way we came back." And now the Fall Classic became a best two-of-three series. The decision to hold back Bumgarner had worked out swimmingly for the Giants skipper.

WORLD SERIES GAME 5

When they led Game 4 by two runs in the fifth, the Royals appeared headed for a comfortable 3-1 lead in the Series. Now, with Bumgarner slated to start Game 5, it seemed likely they would be headed back to Kansas City down 3-2. Of course, not a single player in the KC clubhouse would concede defeat. With their own ace James Shields on the mound, the Boys in Blue were determined to regain the Series lead at AT&T Park.

It was Sunday, October 26th. Twenty-nine years ago on this date the Royals staged a dramatic ninth-inning comeback to win

Game 6 of the 1985 World Series. Facing one of the toughest postseason pitchers in baseball history, could Kansas City again summon some late October magic for an unlikely victory? Three thousand years earlier, a shepherd boy defied the odds to fell a mighty giant with a single stone. Could the Davids in the KC dugout do the same?

Bumgarner took the mound for the first inning. After he dispatched the first two Royals, a glimmer of hope shined through when Lorenzo Cain blooped a single into shallow center. Hosmer struck out to end the inning, but the Royals had proved that the Goliath they faced was in fact human. Perhaps they could break through later on.

Shields, meanwhile, was eager to redeem himself after a rough Game 1 outing. Thus far in the postseason, Big Game James had a big ERA of 7.11. After holding the Giants scoreless in the first, Shields yielded a leadoff single to Hunter "Thorn-in-the-Side" Pence in the second. Belt dropped a bunt that he beat out to put two on with nobody out. The runners advanced on a sac fly by Ishikawa. Taking advantage of an excellent RBI opportunity, Crawford hit a grounder to second that scored a run. The Royals had fallen behind early against MadBum—exactly what they did not want to do.

The untouchable Giant sent Kansas City down in order in the third and again in the fourth. In the bottom of that frame, San Francisco put two on with two out. Crawford again came through for the home team, dumping a single into center. Sandoval hesitated rounding third, but crossed the plate when Dyson had trouble coming up with the ball. The Giants led 2-0. On any other night against any other pitcher, not a catastrophe. On this night, however ...

Benefitting from an Ishikawa misplay, Infante doubled with one out in the fifth. Excitement flickered in the Royals dugout at the prospect of a breakthrough. But by this time, the enemy on the mound had transformed from a mere nine-foot giant into a mighty wizard with a seemingly endless array of malevolent spells. The dark lord summoned his fiendish powers to strike out the next two batters and squash the threat. In the sixth, Kansas City again mounted no offense. The visitors were fast running out of opportunities. Hosmer led off the seventh with a base hit to right, but he would end the inning stranded at first.

Yost brought in Herrera to pitch the seventh. Shields had allowed only two runs through six innings, while striking out four. Normally a solid outing, but on this evening the results seemed woefully inadequate. He-Who-Must-Not-Be-Named cast down three more Royals in the eighth. Bad turned to worse in the bottom of the inning when San Francisco somehow scored three against Herrera and Davis.

Bumgarner took the mound in the ninth with a 5-0 cushion. The margin actually seemed a lot larger, a number more like the national debt. The mesmerizing lefty retired Gordon, Cain, and Hosmer to complete a four-hit shutout.

"He's special, isn't he?" Bochy said afterward about his victorious hurler. Former Giants pitcher Juan Marichal added more detail. "I say that he's cold-blooded," the 1960s ace said. "When he's on the mound, he dominates everybody." With this performance, Bumgarner seemed to be channeling not only Marichal, but also Giants pitching legends Carl Hubbell, Christy Mathewson, and Joe McGinnity rolled into one. MadBum had won all four of his career World Series starts, allowing just one run in 31 innings. The Game 5 battle was over when San Francisco pushed across a run in the second.

The Series war, on the other hand, still raged. Kansas City trailed three games to two, but the action now shifted back to Kauffman Stadium. This was the exact same situation the Royals faced in 1985. "We're looking forward to getting back to our home crowd," Yost said, "where it's going to be absolutely wild and crazy." Dyson concurred. "I feel good about where we're at," the outfielder said. "We don't have to worry about Bumgarner no more."

Sounded good at the time.

WORLD SERIES GAME 6

The Series' return to Kansas City meant the roaring crowd would be wearing blue, not orange. Seagulls would not glide about the ballpark, and Steve Perry would not sing about lights. And in one of the most welcome pieces of good news, Billy Butler would return to the lineup. On the downside, KC had been outscored 16-4 in its last two games. World Series history is replete with the smoking hulks of teams that ran out of gas and got steamrolled in three straight losses to end the Fall Classic. One more defeat and Kansas City would be added to that list. "We've got to walk the tightrope now without a net," Yost said, "but our guys aren't afraid of walking the tightrope without a net."

Game 6 featured a rematch of the starters from Game 2. Jake Peavy sought redemption by pitching his team to the title. Yordano Ventura wanted to extend the season one more game. After the Kansas City Symphony performed the national anthem and Medal of Honor recipient Lieutenant Colonel Charles Hagemeister threw the ceremonial first pitch, the Royals took the field. For the first time since the Wild Card Game a month earlier, they faced elimination.

Ventura dedicated his outing to his friend and fellow Dominican Oscar Taveras, the 22-year-old St. Louis outfielder who had died two days earlier in a car accident. The rookie flamethrower sent the Giants down in order in the first. If he had any nerves about starting an elimination game in the World Series, it did not show early. Peavy surrendered a walk and a single, but similarly retired the Royals without a run.

Gordon started the bottom of the second with a bloop off the end of his bat that dropped in for a hit. Perez lined a single to right to put runners at the corners. With Moustakas stepping to the plate, Kansas City had an opportunity to strike first and take some pressure off its young hurler. Moose delivered a double down the right field line that scored Gordon. After Infante struck out, Escobar tapped a bouncer to the right side and then outraced

Belt to the bag. The runners could not advance, but KC had the bases loaded with just one out. Aoki slapped a single to left to score Perez, and the bases were still loaded. Seeking to avoid an avalanche, Bochy replaced Peavy with Yusmeiro Petit. Cain greeted the reliever by dropping a blooper into right. Two more scored. The barrage continued with Hosmer, who chopped a hit over the drawn-in infield to plate two more. Butler then smoked a drive into right center, scoring Hosmer. Kansas City led 7-0. In just two innings the Boys in Blue had scored the same number of runs they had tallied in all three games in San Francisco.

An inning later, Cain drove in Infante with a ground rule double to center. The Kansas City second baseman scored again in the fifth when Escobar doubled him home. In the seventh, Moustakas crushed a solo shot over the right field wall. It was Moose's fifth home run in October, breaking Willie Aikens's team record of four homers in a single postseason.

Ventura meanwhile rolled along, mowing down Giant after Giant with his blazing fastballs. Despite issuing five walks, he allowed no runs and just three hits over seven innings. The dominating performance perhaps gave Royals fans a glimpse of their ace of the future. Jason Frasor and Tim Collins pitched the final two innings of the 10-0 pounding. The World Series was even at three games apiece.

Days earlier, after Game 4, Yost had revealed a hidden desire: "Oh, man, somewhere inside of me secretly I had hoped that it would go seven games for the excitement and the thrill of it." His hopes were now realized. "I had a very, very strong feeling that whoever won Game 6 was going to win Game 7," said the KC manager, adding to his earlier revelation. History supported his prediction. The previous eight times a home team trailing a World Series 3-2 had won Game 6, all eight teams went on to win Game 7. That list included the 1985 Royals.

Electricity surged from the Kansas City locker room through the city and to the farthest corners of Royals Nation. The anticipation of a world championship—one of the unlikeliest in baseball history—reached a fever pitch. The Boys in Blue were ready. The K would be rocking.

But in the opposing clubhouse an ominous presence lurked. The Orange and Black legion had been battered, but not vanquished. Would the Royals' magic be enough to overcome the foul conjuring of a dark lord?

WORLD SERIES GAME 7

Wednesday, October 29, 2014: Kansas City buzzed with expectation. Across the metropolitan area and the entire Midwest, fans, both longtime and newly-arrived bandwagon jumpers, sported their Royals attire. Blue-clad strangers passing each other in grocery store aisles nodded and said, "One more." Indeed, the longsuffering franchise had arrived at the brink of a summit not reached for nearly three decades.

For this winner-take-all contest, Ned Yost gave the ball to Jeremy Guthrie. Though the right-hander did not have Cy Young credentials like Kansas City's last Game 7 starter, the crafty veteran did win Game 3 of this World Series. Plus, Yost had his H-D-H relievers fully rested. With no more games this season, the skipper could ride his monster longer than usual—maybe even six innings if needed.

On the other side, Bochy faced a major decision. Would he stick with his original plan to start Tim Hudson or would he go with Madison Bumgarner on just two days' rest? The Giants skipper remained wary of the many innings his unhittable ace had already thrown this season. "This guy is human," Bochy said. "I mean, you can't push him that much." Hudson would get the start. But Bochy added that MadBum would be available, if needed. In other words, it was not a question of *if* Bumgarner would pitch in Game 7, but which inning would he appear.

After opera star Joyce DiDonato sang the national anthem, Bret Saberhagen, appropriately enough, threw out the ceremonial first pitch. The 40,000 boisterous fans packed into The K hoped ensuing events would be a repeat of the last time

160

this pitcher threw from this mound in a World Series Game 7. Guthrie raised hopes for such an outcome by retiring the Giants in order in the first. Hudson yielded a walk to Aoki, but matched Guthrie's zero in the bottom of the frame.

Trouble brewed in the top of the second when Guthrie nicked Sandoval in the elbow. Pence followed by grounding a single into left. Belt then pulled a hit into right to load the bases with nobody out. Dread knotted stomachs throughout the ballpark. Michael Morse sliced a drive to the opposite field in right. Aoki gloved it, but the Panda tagged up and scored, while Pence moved to third. The next batter, Crawford, lifted a fly ball to center to plate another run. Guthrie struck out Juan Perez to end the inning with San Francisco up 2-0. Not a good result for KC, but disaster had been averted.

Butler led off the bottom of the second with a hard grounder up the middle for a base hit. Batting sixth in the order, Gordon followed with a drive into the gap in right center. Moving like a runaway Greyhound (the bus, not the dog), Country Breakfast trucked around the bases to score all the way from first. The crowd roared in delight at Gordon's RBI double. A Hudson fastball then drilled Salvador Perez just above the knee, crumpling the catcher into the dirt. After a visit from team trainer Nick Kenney that lasted several minutes, Perez limped to first. The Royals had two on with nobody out. Moustakas lifted a fly ball to left. Timing Juan Perez's catch, Gordon sprinted to third, sliding in safely just ahead of the tag. Batting with a chance to tie the game, Infante delivered. His fly ball to center scored Gordon and knotted the game 2-2. Seeking to continue the rally, Escobar singled to left. Bochy went to his bullpen—an early hook for Hudson, but this was Game 7. Reliever Jeremy Affeldt retired Aoki to end the inning.

Cain led off the bottom of the third by singling to right. Hosmer followed with a hard grounder up the middle that looked certain to give the Royals runners at the corners with nobody out. But second baseman Joe Panik made a diving backhanded stop that he and Crawford turned into a rally-killing double play.

The umpire initially called Hosmer safe at first, but Bochy's replay challenge overturned the call—the first successful manager challenge in World Series history.

In the top of the fourth, Sandoval, the ever-annoying Panda, chopped a bouncer up the middle that he beat out for an infield hit. The equally troublesome Pence followed with a single into center. With two on and nobody out, Belt lofted a fly ball to deep left that advanced Sandoval to third. Hoping to keep the game tied, Yost unleashed the monster. Morse represented the first challenge for Herrera. The fireballing reliever appeared to win the matchup by breaking the DH's bat. But the resulting flare carried to right and dropped in for a hit. Sandoval crossed the plate with the go-ahead run, while Pence moved to third with just one out. Herrera rebounded to strike out Crawford and retire Juan Perez on a ground out.

The score remained 3-2 heading to the bottom of the fifth. To preserve his narrow lead, Bochy summoned the dreadful presence awaiting in his bullpen. In the movie *Major League*, pitcher Ricky Vaughn enters a game with the rock classic "Wild Thing" blaring through the stadium. As the towering Bumgarner stalked toward the mound, the appropriate musical accompaniment would have been the ominous "O Fortuna."

Infante stepped into the batter's box to face the Unhittable One. And then something amazing happened. With wraiths circling overhead amid dark swirling clouds, a shaft of light shined through. Infante somehow bested Bumgarner by lining a single into right. If Frodo could prevail against Mordor in *The Lord of the Rings*, maybe the Royals had a chance against their Sauron. The next batter, Escobar, laid down a bunt to advance the runner to second. More than a few commentators questioned the wisdom of giving up an out here, but Kansas City moved the tying run into scoring position. The decision actually appeared brilliant when Aoki slashed a liner down the left field line—a sure hit, maybe even extra bases. But Juan Perez was well positioned. He hustled to his right to snare the drive and retire Aoki. Cain ended the inning by striking out.

San Francisco put two men on in the sixth, but Herrera kept them from scoring. Bumgarner retired the Royals in order in the bottom of the inning. Wade Davis entered to pitch the seventh and sent down the Giants one-two-three. MadBum matched him. The Panda doubled off Davis in the eighth, but San Francisco could not score. The Royals again got nothing in the bottom of the frame. After Holland retired the Giants in the top of the ninth, Game 7 of the World Series headed to its final half-inning.

Though Bochy had not intended to use his ace more than three innings, how could he remove MadBum now with the championship on the line? Since allowing a hit to Infante in the fifth, Bumgarner had retired twelve straight batters. Bochy sent him out to pitch the bottom of the ninth.

Due to bat for the Royals were Hosmer, Butler, and Gordon—the heart of the order. The towel-waving fans stood and cheered, desperate to inspire one final rally to lift their heroes to the crown. With a 2-2 count, Hosmer swung mightily at Bumgarner's high fastball. If the power-hitting first baseman had made contact, the ball likely would have cleared I-70 and landed somewhere near the Harry S. Truman Library in Independence. But the swing did not connect and Hosmer went down on strikes. Next up was Butler, hoping to deliver one of his patented drives into the gap. He instead fouled out to first. With Kansas City down to its final out, the best-known Royal stepped into the batter's box. Could Alex Gordon break through against a pitcher who had shot down 14 straight? Down 0-1 in the count, Gordon swung, slapping a drive into shallow left center. Thinking the ball would be caught, Bumgarner raised his arm in triumph.

But then … hope returned! The liner dropped in front of Gregor Blanco and bounced past the centerfielder. Forty thousand fans roared as the white sphere rolled all the way to the wall. Gordon rounded first, pounding for second. Left fielder Juan Perez fumbled the ball away on the warning track. Gordon raced toward third. Could he circle the bases and score the tying run?

163

Perez corralled the ball and fired a one-hopper to Crawford in shallow left. Third base coach Mike Jirschele threw up the stop sign. Gordon would hold at third. The Royals had the tying run ninety feet away. The stadium rocked with renewed fervor. Did this improbable season have one final dose of Blue Magic?

Salvador Perez stepped to the plate. He had batted .348 thus far in the World Series, best on his team. He had tagged Bumgarner with a home run in Game 1—the only ballplayer on the planet to own a World Series homer against the Unhittable One. But Perez had been worn down by a long season of 158 starts at catcher. A fastball ramming his leg earlier in this game compounded his aches and pains. In 1988 Dodgers outfielder Kirk Gibson, barely able to walk, won a World Series game with an unlikely ninth-inning home run. A hit here from the hobbled Perez would similarly etch his name in Fall Classic lore.

Perez swung at the first pitch and missed. He laid off the second high fastball to even the count. Perez swung and missed again at another high delivery to fall behind 1-2. The Royals were down to their final strike. The fourth pitch missed high to even the count. With the "Let's Go Royals" chant echoing through the park, Perez fouled off the next pitch. Ice water flowing through his veins, Bumgarner prepared to throw his 68th pitch of the night. It would be the last pitch of the game, the World Series, the 2014 season. The ball streaked toward the plate. Perez stepped forward and whipped his war club around. Wood collided with cowhide …

… and the ball sailed high into the night sky. Millions gasped, aware that the world championship would be decided by this drive. The white sphere soared above the outfield in a lofty arc. The left fielder drifted back to the warning track. He leapt, glove outstretched. But in vain was his effort. The ball cleared the fence, landing in the bullpen for a two-run home run. Kansas City had won the World Series! Fans erupted into a roar that could be heard in Joplin 150 miles away. As Perez limped around third, his teammates waited to mob him at home plate …

If only. It would have been the most dramatic ending to a season in baseball history. The small-market underdogs winning the World Series on a ninth-inning home run from a catcher who could barely walk. ESPN would have immediately started work on the *30 for 30* special. Ken Burns would have devoted a whole new chapter of his epic *Baseball* series to the Royals triumph.

But alas, it was not meant to be. Perez's final drive shot straight up from his bat in a trajectory no batter wants to see. Sandoval (of course it had to be him) drifted into foul territory near the third base dugout and waited. The ball dropped into his glove. San Francisco had won the 2014 World Series.

Just like that, the season was over.

Chapter 14

Coda

Baseball is a cruel mistress—a fact Kansas City fans know all too well. How bitter the memories of 1977 when the Royals, the best team in baseball, watched the despised Yankees score four runs in the final two innings of Game 5 of the ALCS to steal the pennant. Just a year earlier, George Brett rallied Kansas City from a 6-3 deficit to tie the deciding game of the playoffs with one eighth-inning swing of his bat. The hopes of Royals fans soared to unprecedented heights before Chris Chambliss shattered their dreams in the bottom of the ninth. In 1980 the Royals finally reached the World Series, only to blow leads in three different games to the Phillies.

The franchise endured other disappointments. The late homer to Thurman Munson that negated three Brett home runs and lost a game that could have turned around the 1978 ALCS. The September collapse in 2003. Losing Bo Jackson to a football injury. Trading away David Cone.

And now the 2014 World Series. But in the wake of defeat, it should be remembered that the Royals exceeded expectations—by a wide margin. Of course, that did not make the final loss any less painful. The late season charge to reach the playoffs. The impossible comeback against the A's. The unbelievable sweeps of Los Angeles and Baltimore. To rise to such heights and come so close made the pain all the worse when the dream finally died. "It's a very dejected group in there right now," Yost said about his team after Game 7. "They didn't accomplish their goal." John Viril, writing for KC Kingdom, further summarized the heartbreak: "For Royals fans, this loss will hurt today, tomorrow, and will still hurt 30 years from now when we think about it. It will hurt because the 2014 Royals could have won."

WHAT WENT WRONG?

So why didn't the Royals win the World Series? Why did they fall short? Years after the Civil War, somebody asked Confederate General George Pickett to explain why his side lost the Battle of Gettysburg. Which tactic had failed the South? After some consideration, Pickett replied, "I've always thought the Yankees had something to do with it."

In explaining the Royals World Series defeat, the Giants definitely had something to do with it. Or, more specifically, *a Giant*. Volumes of statistics could be analyzed to dissect the result of the 2014 Fall Classic, but the bottom line is San Francisco had the most dominant player on either roster.

Madison Bumgarner pitched 21 innings in the World Series. He allowed just one run for a smothering 0.43 ERA. All the other Giants hurlers combined to pitch 40 innings in the World Series. They allowed 24 runs for a hitter-friendly 5.40 ERA. The Giants were 3-0 in games in which MadBum appeared. They were 1-3 in the other games. Remove Madison Bumgarner from the equation and San Francisco does not win the 2014 World Series.

There is no question that Bumgarner was the decisive factor in the Giants' victory, but what made him so good? It started with his control. The southpaw walked just one batter in his 21 innings against the Royals. In Game 7 he did not walk anybody; he did not even go to a three-ball count on any of the 17 batters he faced that game. This was a pitcher who could put the ball exactly where he wanted.

While Bumgarner's fastball hit the low to mid-90s, it was his slider that gave Kansas City fits. No NL lefty starter had a higher horizontal velocity on his slider when it crossed the plate. The Royals conversely struggled with such pitches. As a team, Kansas City had the third lowest batting average (.091) against fast, late-breaking sliders.

The Royals contributions to Bumgarner's brilliance did not end with their difficulties against his sliders. Time and time again, the Giant lefty went up the ladder, and time and time again KC's hitters swung at the high offerings. In Game 7 he threw 41 pitches out of the strike zone. Kansas City batters chased 44% of these pitches—the highest chase percentage in any of MadBum's 14 postseason appearances. Swinging at bad balls turns a good pitcher into a great pitcher. And it transforms a great pitcher into a legend.

This is not to say that Bumgarner won the World Series single-handedly. He did not make any offensive contributions, nor did his glove win any games. His teammates came through in those departments. Hunter Pence and Pablo Sandoval hammered the ball again and again in key situations. Pence batted .444 (12 for 27) with 5 RBI and the Panda hit .429 (12 for 28) with 4 RBI. Brandon Crawford also delivered for the Giants, batting .304 with 4 RBI. In the field, Joe Panik made the defensive play of the Series when his backhanded stop in Game 7 turned a potential first-and-third-with-nobody-out situation into a double play. Buster Posey and the Giant pitchers, moreover, limited KC to just one stolen base, neutralizing a major Royals weapon.

As for Kansas City, the team played well. Aside from the lack of stolen bases, the Royals featured their type of baseball. The defense was solid as usual. H-D-H continued their dominance, allowing just two earned runs over 14.2 innings. And in only one game did a Kansas City starter surrender more than three runs. The Royals hit the ball too. Perez, Butler,

Infante, Escobar, and Cain all batted over .300 in the World Series. Infante, Hosmer, Cain, and Perez combined to drive in 17 runs.

Even the punching bag Ned Yost cannot be blamed for the loss. Should he have pulled Guthrie sooner in Game 7? Maybe, but it was just the fourth inning. Perhaps the most controversial decision of the night was Escobar's sacrifice bunt in the fifth inning. The way Bumgarner was pitching though, would allowing the shortstop to swing away have made a difference? We will never know. The decisions of any losing manager can and will be second-guessed, but the moves that worked out must also be considered. Yost's maneuverings in Game 3, for example, helped his team win a tight contest. Without that victory, there is no Game 7.

In sum, the Royals put forth a good effort. Good enough to win a World Series even. They just had the misfortune of facing a dominant pitcher on one of the hottest postseason streaks in baseball history.

TO SEND OR NOT TO SEND

One question did linger in the Game 7 aftermath. Should Alex Gordon have tried to score in the ninth inning? Websites and sports talk shows lit up following the game with debates over this issue. A sizeable contingent, including Kansas governor Sam Brownback, argued that Jirschele should have given Gordon the green light to try to score. A case bolstered by the after-the-fact knowledge of how things played out. Of course, when the decision had to be made, nobody, not Jirschele, not Gordon, not even Bumgarner knew what would happen in either scenario. And that is how any analysis of this decision has to be made. *What did Jirschele know at the time he threw up the stop sign?*

Consider the factors supporting a green light. First, Bumgarner had retired 14 straight batters before Gordon's hit. What were the odds of him giving up two hits in a row? Second, the next batter, Salvador Perez, was worn down and hobbled after a grueling season in which he had batted just .229 after the All-Star Break. Could he deliver a quality at-bat against such a dominant pitcher? Third, the Giants had already made two miscues on this play. With the pressure on the fielders already high, might sending Gordon have forced a third mistake?

There is really only one argument supporting the decision to hold Gordon at third. And that argument is: *He would have been thrown out by 20 feet if he had tried to score!* After stumbling slightly at second, Gordon reached third base about the same time Giants shortstop Brandon Crawford caught the ball in shallow left. Only a bad throw or a misplay by the catcher would have allowed the run to score. Crawford had a strong, accurate arm—he was fourth in the National League in assists in 2014 and he had played quarterback for his high school football team. Buster Posey was a former MVP, one of the best catchers in the league. Considering that Crawford made a throwing error just once every 140 innings during the season and Posey had a .994 fielding percentage as a catcher, the chances of an error were not great. At best there is a 2% possibility Gordon scores.

Meaning there is at least a 98% chance he gets cut down at the plate to end the World Series. And then the criticisms heaped on Jirschele would have been relentless. How do you deny Perez the chance to drive in the tying run? He delivered the game-winning hit in the Wild Card Game. He was batting .348 in the World Series, the highest on his team at the time. He had two hits in this Series against Bumgarner, including a home run. Plus, MadBum could have been tiring. Heading into the final at-bat he had thrown more than 60 pitches, just three days after throwing 117 pitches in Game 5. He could have hung a fat slider to Perez.

Second-guessing and wondering *what if* are time-honored traditions in all sports. So it is no surprise that the ninth-inning stop sign received such scrutiny. But the evidence overwhelmingly reveals that the Royals had a far greater chance to score the tying run by holding Gordon at third than by sending him on a desperate dash to the plate with little chance of success.

Mike Jirschele made the right call.

A MAGICAL SEASON

The day after Game 7, the team held a postseason rally at Kauffman Stadium to honor the players. More than 10,000 fans, including Kansas City mayor Sly James, attended to show their appreciation for what the Boys in Blue had accomplished. With time for reflection, both players and fans found much to celebrate in what had been an amazing season. Royals fan Ken Breiner expressed a common sentiment among those in attendance when he said, "We still love the Royals and I'll never stop loving them." The players and team officials, as well as David Glass, returned these feelings to the KC faithful. "Without you, none of this is possible," the owner said, "so thank you for hanging in there with us."

Billy Butler, the longest-tenured Royal, reflected on how far the franchise had come. "To see this thing go from step one to where we are now," the DH said, "I couldn't be more honored to be part of this organization." Ned Yost expressed his appreciation of his players. "I don't think I've ever been as proud of anything in my life as I have been of this team and the way they performed this postseason."

The 2014 run had indeed revitalized a fan base. After so many years of drought and suffering, Royals Nation again surged with energy. Kansas City had reached the World Series for just the third time in franchise history. The Royals' first two Series appearances came during a ten-year span of winning and frequent playoff appearances. Special achievements to be sure, but the run in 2014 shocked the world. Not far removed from its fourth straight 90-loss season, the team blazed into the postseason and set a major league record with eight consecutive playoff victories. Kansas City came alive in a way not seen for three decades.

After the Royals won the American League pennant, Joe Posnanski posted a quote from the late KC baseball legend Buck O'Neil. "I don't like that word unbelievable," the longtime Monarch said, "… nothing is unbelievable." In 2014 the team representing his beloved home city proved these words true.

WAIT TILL NEXT YEAR

At the rally after the World Series, Jackson County Executive Mike Sanders reminded fans, "It's only 158 days to Opening Day." Indeed, the 2014 season, like every baseball season, will fade into memory. A new season will begin and all the teams will return to the same position at the starting gate. New heroes, new goats, new stories, and new magic will follow.

So what type of significance will the Royals World Series run hold for the team's future? Will 2014 mark the start of another golden age, a la 1976? Or will it be a short-lived oasis in a desert of mediocre seasons—something like a more successful version of 2003?

Boding well for the former is the return of most of the team's core offensive and defensive contributors. Gordon, Hosmer, Moustakas, Cain, Dyson, Perez, Escobar, and Infante are back in 2015. So too are starting pitchers Ventura, Vargas, Guthrie, and Duffy. Despite the attempts of opposing GMs, the Three-Headed Monster returns as well. And this time the Boys in Blue start the season as battle-tested veterans, refined in the fiery crucible of postseason action. Recalling the dramatic comeback in the Wild Card Game, Yost observed, "Something clicked, and from that moment on, these guys were immune from any type of pressure or any situation." The manager continued by adding, "You have to walk through that door knowing you're gonna win that game that day, and these guys have it."

Kansas City, however, did lose key components from its pennant-winning squad. Longtime Royal Billy Butler signed a free agent deal with Oakland. The news saddened his legions of fans who will miss watching him play, as well as his estimable charity work in the community. Needing a designated hitter, Moore added former Mariner Kendrys Morales. The Royals also did not re-sign James Shields, instead acquiring starters Edinson Volquez and Kris Medlen to fill out the rotation. And former Ranger Alex Rios replaces Nori Aoki in the outfield. Losing the production and clubhouse presence of Shields, Butler, and Aoki hurts, but their replacements have the potential to make significant contributions of their own.

Of course, baseball never remains in stasis. Each team adds and subtracts personnel. Some players improve, some players decline. Nobody knows what will happen until the games are played. The Royals could tear through the competition in '15, winning the first of three straight world championships. Or injuries could strike, knocking Kansas City out of contention by July. But regardless of future outcomes, the accomplishments of the 2014 Royals will never be forgotten. Breaking the shackles of a decades-long dark age, the team captivated a nation with its historic October run. Previously unheralded players emerged as heroes, electrifying a city with their feats on fields of green. A team expected to do little, charged all the way to Game 7 of the World Series. Royals faithful no longer need harken all the way back to 1985 to find glory days on which to reflect. The year 2014 is now indelibly etched in franchise annals. One of the finest groups of ballplayers ever to represent Kansas City left it all out on the field. An epic campaign that ended just ninety feet short of the ultimate goal. For Royals fans, the season showcased baseball at its best, when the competition elevates from spectacle to soul-stirring drama. The unfolding diamond events sparked exhilaration from even the most stoic of adults, while inspiring the dreams of countless children staging their own Game 7s in the backyard. For the Royals players, who once were those children in the backyard, the dream became reality. And while the memories will be treasured, the near miss further stoked the competitive fires within. These Men in Blue now know firsthand what is possible.

As Alex Gordon said, looking ahead: "This Spring Training we have something to work for, we have one more run we need to score."

Acknowledgements

I wish to thank Jodi Fuson for proofreading this book and providing many helpful comments. Thank you also to Annie Pratt of USA TODAY Sports Images for her valuable assistance. I furthermore remain grateful to Benjamin G. Rader, Ron Kalkwarf, and Tania Kruce for their help.

Finally, thank you to my wife Jill for her MVP-level contributions to *Ninety Feet Away* and all my writings.

Sources

Chapter 1

• Associated Press, "Royals eliminate A's on Salvador Perez's walk-off single in 12th," ESPN.com, September 30, 2014, http://scores.espn.go.com/mlb/recap?gameId=340930107

• Sam Mellinger, "These Royals are eager to include their fans in this long-awaited moment," *The Kansas City Star*, October 7, 2014, http://www.kansascity.com/sports/spt-columns-blogs/sam-mellinger/article2535406.html

• Tim Rohan, "Ned Yost, the Royals' Rugged Leader, Looks Inward," *The New York Times*, September 24, 2014, http://www.nytimes.com/2014/09/25/sports/baseball/ned-yost-the-royals-rugged-leader-looks-inward.html

• John Perrotto, "Oft-criticized manager Ned Yost keeps Royals winning," *USA Today*, October 20, 2014, http://www.usatoday.com/story/sports/mlb/royals/2014/10/19/ned-yost-kansas-city-royals-manager-world-series-san-francisco-giants/17589265/

• Pat Borzi, "Yost's Bad Week Leads to the Brewers' Elimination," *The New York Times*, September 29, 2007, http://www.nytimes.com/2007/09/29/sports/baseball/29brewers.html

• Paul Sullivan, "Improbably, Ned Yost has Royals in the World Series," *Chicago Tribune*, October 15, 2014, http://www.chicagotribune.com/sports/breaking/ct-sullivan-baseball-spt-1016-20141015-story.html

Chapter 2

• Peter C. Bjarkman, *Encyclopedia of Major League Baseball: American League* (New York: Carroll & Graf, 1993), 183-198, 328-333.

• Steve Cameron, *Moments, Memories, Miracles: a Quarter Century with the Kansas City Royals* (Dallas: Taylor, 1992), 87-106, 138-152.

• Nick Acocella, "Finley entertained and enraged," ESPN Classic, http://espn.go.com/classic/biography/s/Finley_Charles.html

• Jared Diamond and Kevin Helliker, "Think the Kansas City Royals are Named for Kings? That's a Bunch of Bull," *The Wall Street Journal*, October 16, 2014, http://www.wsj.com/articles/did-you-know-the-kansas-city-royals-were-named-after-cows-not-kings-1413426602

• Frank White with Bill Althaus, *One Man's Dream: My Town, My Team, My Time.* (Olathe, KS: Ascend Books, 2012), 78, 89

• Associated Press, "Brett in Hospital for Surgery," *The New York Times*, March 1, 1981, http://www.nytimes.com/1981/03/01/sports/brett-in-hospital-for-surgery.html

Chapter 3

• Peter C. Bjarkman, *Encyclopedia of Major League Baseball: American League* (New York: Carroll & Graf, 1993), 199-200.

• Steve Cameron, *Moments, Memories, Miracles: a Quarter Century with the Kansas City Royals* (Dallas: Taylor, 1992), 157-166.

• Mark Stallard, *Legacy of Blue: 45 Years of Kansas City Royals History & Trivia* (Overland Park, KS: Kaw Valley Books, 2014), 58-65, 76.

• Craig Brown, "Today in Royals History: David Glass is Approved," *Royals Review*, April 17, 2013, http://www.royalsreview.com/2013/4/17/4233412/today-in-royals-history-david-glass-is-approved

• Art Stewart, *The Art of Scouting: Seven Decades Chasing Hopes and Dreams in Major League Baseball* (Olathe, KS: Ascend Books, 2014), 139.

• Joe Posnanski, "SI Vault: Royals, Flush: How Kansas City built a team to be envied," *Sports Illustrated*, October 19, 2014, http://www.si.com/mlb/2014/10/19/si-vault-kansas-city-royals-world-series-joe-posnanski

• David Schoenfield, "Royals' Latino Players make huge impact," ESPN.com, October 15, 2014, http://espn.go.com/blog/sweetspot/post/_/id/52660/royals-latino-players-make-huge-impact

• Hal Bodley, "Fan-turned-GM hopes to restore Royals' majesty," *USA Today*, June 10, 2006, http://usatoday30.usatoday.com/sports/baseball/columnist/bodley/2006-06-08-bodley-royals_x.htm?

• Sam Mellinger, "The Royals' journey from a joke to the World Series," *The Kansas City Star*, October 18, 2014, http://www.kansascity.com/sports/spt-columns-blogs/sam-mellinger/article3014456.html

• Sam Walton, *Made in America* (New York: Bantam Books, 1992), 196-197.

• Steve Wulf, "Echoes of the '85 K.C. Royals," ESPN.com, October 22, 2014, http://espn.go.com/mlb/story/_/id/11743096/29-reasons-care-1985-kansas-city-royals

• "2015 Kansas City Royals compensation," *Baseball Prospectus*, http://www.baseballprospectus.com/compensation/?team=KCA

Chapter 4

• "Major Winter Storm February 4-5, 2014," National Weather Service Kansas City/Pleasant Hill, MO Weather Forecast Office, February 5, 2014, http://www.crh.noaa.gov/eax/?n=140204winterstorm

• Zachary D. Rymer, "Does Kansas City Royals' Promising Spring Hint at Breakout Season in 2014?" *Bleacher Report*, March 24, 2014, http://bleacherreport.com/articles/2004087-does-kansas-city-royals-promising-spring-hint-at-breakout-season-in-2014#articles/

• Jim Bowden and Casey Stern, "Kansas City Royals – MLB Network Radio Spring Training Tour 2014," SiriusXM Sports, March 5, 2014, http://www.youtube.com/watch?v=-q1VH_JCfjM

• Andy McCullough, "Royals' Luke Hochevar to have Tommy John surgery," *The Kansas City Star*, March 7, 2014, http://www.kansascity.com/sports/mlb/kansas-city-royals/article341613/Royals%E2%80%99-Luke-Hochevar-to-have-Tommy-John-surgery.html

• "MLB Team Stats – 2013," ESPN.com, http://espn.go.com/mlb/stats/team/_/stat/batting/year/2013/league/al

• Anthony Riccobono, "MLB Betting Odds: Dodgers, Tigers Expected To Reach 2014 World Series?" *International Business Times*, February 11, 2014, http://www.ibtimes.com/mlb-betting-odds-dodgers-tigers-expected-reach-2014-world-series-1554762

• Rick Montgomery, "With the Royals in the World Series, Kansas City is a baseball town again," *The Kansas City Star*, October 20, 2014, http://www.kansascity.com/sports/mlb/kansas-city-royals/article3190800.html

• Associated Press, "Alex Gonzalez singles in 9th to lift Tigers past Royals," ESPN.com, March 31, 2014, http://scores.espn.go.com/mlb/recap?id=340331106

• Associated Press, "Alex Gordon matches career high with 4 RBIs as Royals drop Rays," ESPN.com, April 9, 2014, http://scores.espn.go.com/mlb/recap?gameId=340409107

• ESPN.com news services, "Omar Infante takes pitch to face," ESPN.com, April 8, 2014, http://espn.go.com/mlb/story/_/id/10747075/

• Ben Reiter, "As Royals thrive, Alex Gordon emerges as dark-horse MVP candidate," *Sports Illustrated*, August 20, 2014, http://www.si.com/mlb/2014/08/20/alex-gordon-kansas-city-royals-mvp-candidate

• "Alex Gordon BIO," University of Nebraska Athletic Department, 2015, http://www.huskers.com/ViewArticle.dbml?ATCLID=5469

• Bob Nightengale, "Royals demote draft-bust Gordon to minors; switch from 3B to left field," *USA Today*, May 3, 2010, http://content.usatoday.com/communities/dailypitch/post/2010/05/royals-demote-3b-draft-bust-gordon-to-minors-switch-to-left-field/1

• Dick Kaegel, "Gordon's work ethic stems from Mom," MLB.com, May 9, 2014, http://m.royals.mlb.com/news/article/74707962/royals-alex-gordons-work-ethic-stems-from-mom

• Doug Tucker, "Hard work finally pays off for Royals' Alex Gordon," *USA Today*, April 22, 2011, http://usatoday30.usatoday.com/sports/baseball/al/2011-04-21-2780797190_x.htm

• Dirk Chatelain, "Alex Gordon: A path to stardom out of left field," *Omaha World-Herald*, July 13, 2014 http://dataomaha.com/documents/alex-gordon-a-path-to-stardom-out-of-left-field

• Alan Matthews, "High School Player of the Year: Mike Moustakas," *Baseball America*, July 2, 2007, http://www.baseballamerica.com/today/high-school/awards/player-of-the-year/2007/264412.html

• Dick Kaegel, "Big-hitting Moustakas is wise beyond years," MLB.com, March 1, 2011, http://m.mlb.com/news/article/16779370/

• Jorge L. Ortiz, "Get to know: Mike Moustakas heating up for the hot corner in Kansas City," *USA Today*, March 27, 2011, http://content.usatoday.com/communities/dailypitch/post/2011/03/get-to-know-mike-moustakas-heating-up-for-the-hot-corner-in-kansas-city/1

• Arash Markazi, "Moustakas' big blast propels Royals," ESPN.com, October 3, 2014, http://espn.go.com/mlb/playoffs/2014/story/_/id/11632350/mike-moustakas-home-run-lifts-kansas-city-royals-huge-win

• "Billy Butler Signs NLI with Florida Baseball," University of Florida Athletic Department, 2003, http://www.gatorzone.com/baseball/misc.php?p=release/butler

• Barry M. Bloom, "Royals' Butler named Futures MVP," MLB.com, July 9, 2006, http://m.mlb.com/news/article/1549647/

• Dick Kaegel, "Royals send Butler back to Triple-A," MLB.com, May 29, 2008, http://m.royals.mlb.com/news/article/2794247/

• Jeff Zillgitt, "Big Floridian bashes homers, weighs options," *USA Today*, April 10, 2008, http://usatoday30.usatoday.com/sports/preps/baseball/2008-04-09-Hosmer_N.htm

• Dick Kaegel, "Royals' top pick remains unsigned," MLB.com, August 13, 2008 http://m.mlb.com/news/article/3302679/

• Associated Press, "Super-prospect Eric Hosmer debuts," ESPN.com, May 6, 2011, http://sports.espn.go.com/mlb/news/story?id=6495925

• Tyler Kepner, "Royals Have an Emerging Star Without a Supernova Salary," *The New York Times*, March 29, 2012, http://www.nytimes.com/2012/03/30/sports/baseball/royals-hosmer-an-emerging-star-without-the-star-salary.html

• Sam Mellinger, "Confident Eric Hosmer carries Royals down stretch," *The Kansas City Star*, September 21, 2013, http://www.kansascity.com/sports/mlb/kansas-city-royals/article327964/Confident-Eric-Hosmer-carries-Royals-down-stretch.html

Chapter 5

• Dick Kaegel, "Mom's support has Perez on Royals' fast track," MLB.com, September 22, 2011, http://m.royals.mlb.com/news/article/25066304/

• Dick Kaegel, "Perez, catcher of the future, called on by Royals," MLB.com, August 10, 2011, http://m.mlb.com/news/article/23018106/

• Associated Press, "Royals' Perez has surgery to repair torn meniscus," *USA Today*, March 16, 2012, http://usatoday30.usatoday.com/sports/baseball/al/2012-03-16-2998742228_x.htm

• Tyler Kepner, "Lights, Catcher, Action!" *The New York Times*, October 21, 2014, http://www.nytimes.com/2014/10/22/sports/baseball/world-series-2014-kansas-city-royals-catcher-salvador-perez-perfume.html?_r=1

• Tyler Kepner, "How a Disgruntled Ace Gave the Royals a Full House," *The New York Times*, October 11, 2014, http://www.nytimes.com/2014/10/12/sports/baseball/how-a-disgruntled-ace-gave-the-royals-a-full-house-.html?_r=0

• Adam McCalvy, "Brewers add Greinke in deal with Royals," MLB.com, December 19, 2010, http://m.mlb.com/news/article/16345284/

• Andy McCullough, "A late bloomer, Royals outfielder Lorenzo Cain making up for lost time," *The Kansas City Star*, May 23, 2014, http://www.kansascity.com/sports/mlb/kansas-city-royals/article402287/A-late-bloomer-Royals-outfielder-Lorenzo-Cain-making-up-for-lost-time.html

• Bob Dutton, "Lorenzo Cain put on disabled list in series of KC roster moves," *The Kansas City Star*, August 10, 2013, http://www.kansascity.com/sports/mlb/kansas-city-royals/article325015/Lorenzo-Cain-put-on-disabled-list-in-series-of-KC-roster-moves.html

• Andy McCullough, "Royals send Mike Moustakas down to Class AAA Omaha," *The Kansas City Star*, May 22, 2014, http://www.kansascity.com/sports/mlb/kansas-city-royals/article396240/Royals-send-Mike-Moustakas-down-to-Class-AAA-Omaha.html

• "Yordano Ventura leaves in third," ESPN.com, May 26, 2014, http://espn.go.com/mlb/story/_/id/10986858/yordano-ventura-kansas-city-royals-leaves-start-elbow-discomfort

• Gene Guidi, "20-year-old Venezuelan prospect dealing with death threats," *Houston Chronicle*, February 20, 2002, http://www.chron.com/sports/astros/article/20-year-old-Venezuelan-prospect-dealing-with-2067284.php

• John Sickels, "Prospect Retrospective: Omar Infante, 2B, Kansas City Royals," SB Nation, December 14, 2013, http://www.minorleagueball.com/2013/12/14/5209956/royals-sign-omar-infante-free-agent-prospect-retrospective

• Associated Press, "Edwin Encarnacion matches AL record for HRs in May with 16th," ESPN.com, May 29, 2014, http://scores.espn.go.com/mlb/recap?gameId=340529114

• Stuart Wallace, "Yordano Ventura's (Pitcher's) elbow: Valgus Extension Overload," SB Nation, May 30, 2014, http://www.beyondtheboxscore.com/2014/5/30/5759720/yordano-venturas-pitchers-elbow-valgus-extension-overload-syndrome-injury

• Connor Moylan, "The Royals keep screwing their fans," Royals Review, May 29, 2014, http://www.royalsreview.com/royals-editorial-opinion-reaction/2014/5/29/5760046/the-growing-disconnect

• Joe Posnanski, "The hardest team to love," HardballTalk, May 27, 2014, http://hardballtalk.nbcsports.com/2014/05/27/the-hardest-team-to-love/

Chapter 6

• Cary Osborne, "Hart graduate James Shields: Best yet to come?" *The Santa Clarita Valley Signal*, March 12, 2012, http://www.signalscv.com/archives/61519/

• Robbie Knopf, "James Shields, The Best Draft Pick in Rays History," FanSided, December 12, 2012, http://rayscoloredglasses.com/2012/12/12/james-shields-the-best-draft-pick-in-rays-history/

• Michael Rosenberg, "Mocked at time, Royals' trade for Shields now looks like a master move," *Sports Illustrated*, October 20, 2014, http://www.si.com/mlb/2014/10/20/james-shields-trade-royals-rays-wil-myers-dayton-moore

• Matthew Peters, "Apple Valley grad Jason Vargas on a wild ride to the World Series," *Victorville Daily Press*, October 20, 2014, http://www.vvdailypress.com/article/20141020/Sports/141029978

• Andy McCullough, "Jason Vargas brings calm approach to Royals' starting rotation," *The Kansas City Star*, May 16, 2014, http://www.kansascity.com/sports/mlb/kansas-city-royals/article343882/Jason-Vargas-brings-calm-approach-to-Royals%E2%80%99-starting-rotation.html

• Vahe Gregorian, "A Journey to the Launch Point of the Royals' rocket arm," *The Kansas City Star*, January 23, 2015, http://projects.kansascity.com/2015/becoming-yordano/#7955736

• Zachary D. Rymer, "Introducing MLB Fans to Yordano Ventura, Baseball's Next Pitching Phenom," Bleacher Report, March 19, 2014, http://bleacherreport.com/articles/1999051-introducing-mlb-fans-to-yordano-ventura-baseballs-next-pitching-phenom

• Associated Press, "How can you explain Yordano Ventura's 100 mph pitches? Scientists break down young Royals ace," *New York Daily News*, May 26, 2014, http://www.nydailynews.com/sports/baseball/kansas-city-ace-ventura-blowing-batters-article-1.1805930

• Associated Press, "Astros win fourth straight, but George Springer's homer streak ends," ESPN.com, May 27, 2014, http://scores.espn.go.com/mlb/recap?gameId=340527107

• Joe Zavala, "Ashland High School alumnus gives $650,000 toward field," *Mail Tribune* (Medford, Oregon), October 3, 2014, http://www.mailtribune.com/article/20141003/News/141009848

• Erik Malinowski, "For Royals' Guthrie, World Series road has been long, winding mission," FOXSports, October 24, 2014, http://www.msn.com/en-us/sports/mlb/for-royals-guthrie-world-series-road-has-been-long-winding-mission/ar-BBaRgic?

• Adam Kilgore, "Jeremy Guthrie's long path to Game 7," *The Washington Post*, October 29, 2014, http://www.washingtonpost.com/news/sports/wp/2014/10/29/jeremy-guthries-long-path-to-game-7/

• Albert Chen, "Royals turn to Jeremy Guthrie, their man on a mission, for Game 7," *Sports Illustrated*, October 29, 2014, http://www.si.com/mlb/2014/10/29/jeremy-guthrie-world-series-game-7-kansas-city-royals-san-francisco-giants

• Dick Kaegel, "Duffy taking leave from baseball," MLB.com, March 24, 2010, http://m.royals.mlb.com/news/article/8893758/

• Dick Kaegel, "Duffy credits his mother for success on hill," MLB.com, May 11, 2012, http://m.royals.mlb.com/news/article/30748372/
• Dick Kaegel, "Duffy takes second opportunity in stride," MLB.com, February 25, 2011, http://m.royals.mlb.com/news/article/16733940/
• Danny Wild, "Royals prospect Duffy returns to club," MiLB.com, June 2, 2010, http://indianapolis.indians.milb.com/news/article.jsp?ymd=20100602&content_id=10730444&vkey=news_milb&fext=.jsp
• Associated Press, "Two on Royals to get Tommy John," ESPN.com, May 18, 2012, http://espn.go.com/mlb/story/_/id/7947423/kansas-city-royals-danny-duffy-blake-wood-headed-tommy-john-surgery
• Lawr Michaels, "Prospect watch: Royals' Duffy a classic post-hype sleeper," *USA Today*, April 19, 2014, http://www.usatoday.com/story/sports/fantasy/baseball/2014/04/17/prospect-watch-danny-duffy-mookie-betts-joey-gallo/7826251/

Chapter 7

• Associated Press, "Nori Aoki (groin strain) goes to DL," ESPN.com, June 21, 2014, http://espn.go.com/mlb/story/_/id/11116185/kansas-city-royals-place-nori-aoki-15-day-disabled-list
• Marc Carig, "Raul Ibanez's work ethic fueled his success and he hopes it continues," *The Star-Ledger*, April 15, 2012, http://www.nj.com/yankees/index.ssf/2012/04/raul_ibanezs_work_ethic_fueled.html
• Paul White, "Phillies veteran Raul Ibanez, 36, hits his stride in Philadelphia," *USA Today*, May 29, 2009, http://usatoday30.usatoday.com/sports/baseball/nl/phillies/2009-05-28-raul-Ibanez_N.htm
• "Raul Ibanez signs with Seattle," MLB.com, December 26, 2012, http://m.mariners.mlb.com/news/article/40790732/
• ESPN Stats & Information, "Ibanez has a knack for the dramatic," ESPN.com, October 11, 2012, http://espn.go.com/blog/statsinfo/post/_/id/53182/Ibanez-has-a-knack-for-the-dramatic
• Associated Press, "Tigers blow out second-place Royals in 16-4 romp," ESPN.com, July 10, 2014, http://scores.espn.go.com/mlb/recap?id=340710107
• Associated Press, "Rick Porcello ties for MLB lead in wins as Tigers get 5th straight victory," ESPN.com, July 12, 2014, http://scores.espn.go.com/mlb/recap?id=340712107
• "MLB Team Stats – 2014," ESPN.com, http://espn.go.com/mlb/stats/team/_/stat/batting/split/181/type/expanded
• Dick Kaegel, "Adversity, obstacles no match for mighty Dyson," MLB.com, May 12, 2014, http://m.royals.mlb.com/news/article/75209290/adversity-obstacles-no-match-for-mighty-kansas-city-royals-outfielder-jarrod-dyson

• Andy McCullough, "Jarrod Dyson is the Royals' engine who could," *The Kansas City Star*, October 18, 2014, http://www.kansascity.com/sports/mlb/kansas-city-royals/article3005416.html
• "Royals' Perez, Holland, Gordon selected to All-Star game," *The Topeka Capital-Journal*, July 6, 2014, http://cjonline.com/sports/2014-07-06/royals-perez-holland-gordon-selected-all-star-game
• Associated Press, "Royals' Gordon to miss All-Star game with injury," *USA Today*, July 11, 2014, http://www.usatoday.com/story/sports/mlb/2014/07/10/royals-gordon-to-miss-all-star-game-with-injury/12498081/
• Andy McCullough, "Salvador Perez faced tough challenges in All-Star Game," *The Kansas City Star*, July 16, 2014, http://www.kansascity.com/sports/mlb/kansas-city-royals/article736523.html
• Bob Nightengale, "Royals' Raul Ibanez give teammates goosebumps," *USA Today*, September 9, 2014, http://www.usatoday.com/story/sports/mlb/2014/09/08/raul-Ibanez-impact-on-royals-clubhouse/15314435/
• Andy McCullough, "Royals, in part because of financial constraints, stand pat at trade deadline as Dave Price joins Tigers," *The Kansas City Star*, July 31, 2014, http://www.kansascity.com/sports/mlb/kansas-city-royals/article840864.html
• Andy McCullough, "Royals trade Danny Valencia to Toronto, recall Christian Colon," The Kansas City Star, July 29, 2014, http://www.kansascity.com/sports/mlb/kansas-city-royals/article821128.html

Chapter 8

• Associated Press, "Escobar, Ventura lead Royals past Twins, 6-3," ESPN.com, July 31, 2014, http://scores.espn.go.com/mlb/recap?gameId=340731107
• David Brown, "Royals' Jarrod Dyson does 'first-place' backflip after catching last out," Yahoo Sports, August 11, 2014, http://sports.yahoo.com/blogs/mlb-big-league-stew/royals-outfielder-jarrod-dyson-does--first-place--backflip-after-making-catch-for-last-out-025840860.html
• Jackson Alexander, "Korea's Royals superfan gets boisterous welcome," MLB.com, August 11, 2014, http://m.royals.mlb.com/news/article/89143378/koreas-royals-superfan-sungwoo-lee-gets-boisterous-welcome
• Jay Jaffe, "Anatomy of a surprise champion: How the Royals won the American League," *Sports Illustrated*, October 17, 2014, http://www.si.com/mlb/2014/10/16/kansas-city-royals-american-league-pennant-world-series
• "Top 100 Royals: #46 Kelvin Herrera," Royals Authority, June 2, 2014, http://www.royalsauthority.com/top-100-royals-98-kelvin-herrera-%E2%88%99-rhp-%E2%88%99-2011-present/
• John Sickels, "Prospect of the Day: Kelvin Herrera, RHP, Kansas City Royals," SB Nation, September 27, 2011, http://www.minorleagueball.com/2011/9/27/2451743/prospect-of-the-day-kelvin-herrera-rhp-kansas-city-royals

• Bill Madden, "World Series Confidential: Royals bullpen keeps Giants off board in Game 2," *New York Daily News*, October 23, 2014, http://www.nydailynews.com/sports/baseball/madden-world-series-confidential-royals-pen-mightier-article-1.1984167

• Joel Wagler, "Wad Davis and Kelvin Herrera Magnificent For Kansas City Royals," KC Kingdom, October 6, 2014, http://kckingdom.com/2014/10/06/wade-davis-kelvin-herrera-magnificent-kansas-city-royals/

• Andy McCullough, "Royals star reliever Wade Davis carries memory of stepbrother on the mound," *The Kansas City Star*, August 16, 2014, http://www.kansascity.com/sports/mlb/kansas-city-royals/article1235503.html

• Barry Svrluga, "Was the 'James Shields-Wil Myers deal' really the 'Wade Davis trade'?" *The Washington Post*, October 15, 2014, http://www.washingtonpost.com/news/sports/wp/2014/10/15/was-the-james-shields-wil-myers-deal-really-the-wade-davis-trade/

• Jeff Passan, "Wade Davis, a fishing pond and the story of a guy who wanted to be great at something," Yahoo Sports, October 24, 2014, http://sports.yahoo.com/news/wade-davis--a-fishing-pond-and-the-story-of-a-guy-who-wanted-to-be-great-at-something-040248816.html

• Vahe Gregorian, "Royals' Holland stays true to roots after improbable rise," *The Kansas City Star*, June 3, 2014, http://www.kansascity.com/sports/spt-columns-blogs/vahe-gregorian/article445083/Royals%E2%80%99-Holland-stays-true-to-roots-after-improbable-rise.html

• Keith Jarrett, "An October to remember for Greg Holland," *Asheville Citizen-Times*, October 18, 2014, http://www.citizen-times.com/story/sports/2014/10/18/october-remember-greg-holland/17499337/

• Mike Axisa, "Marlins gamble on Aaron Crow's upside helping already stacked 'pen," CBSSports.com, November 28, 2014, http://www.cbssports.com/mlb/eye-on-baseball/24846649/marlins-gamble-on-aaron-crows-upside-helping-already-stacked-pen

• ESPN.com news services, "Royals add Jason Frasor to pen," ESPN.com, July 16, 2014, http://espn.go.com/mlb/story/_/id/11223260/kansas-city-royals-add-bullpen-trade-texas-rangers-rhp-jason-frasor

• Andy McCullough, "Lefty reliever Francisley Bueno, now healthy, poised to rejoin Royals," June 3, 2014, http://www.kansascity.com/sports/mlb/kansas-city-royals/article444121/Lefty-reliever-Francisley-Bueno-now-healthy-poised-to-rejoin-Royals.html

• Associated Press, "Kratz, Vargas lead Royals over Twins 6-4," ESPN.com, August 18, 2014, http://scores.espn.go.com/mlb/recap?id=340818109

• Associated Press, "Infante has 3 doubles to lead Royals past Rockies," ESPN.com, August 19, 2014, http://scores.espn.go.com/mlb/recap?id=340819127

• Associated Press, "Royals turn back Twins on Alex Gordon's 2-run homer in ninth," ESPN.com, Aug 26, 2014, http://scores.espn.go.com/mlb/recap?gameId=340826107

Chapter 9

• Associated Press, "Royals ride James Shields, big Yankees error in third to victory," ESPN.com, Sept 5, 2014, http://scores.espn.go.com/mlb/recap?gameId=340905110
• Associated Press, "Royals active Eric Hosmer," ESPN.com, September 1, 2014, http://espn.go.com/mlb/story/_/id/11448386/kansas-city-royals-activate-eric-hosmer-amid-many-moves
• Andy McCullough, "Pitcher Brandon Finnegan impresses Royals after call-up, could open 2015 in big leagues," *The Kansas City Star*, September 24, 2014, http://www.kansascity.com/sports/mlb/kansas-city-royals/article2235581.html
• Andy McCullough, "Meet the fastest man in baseball: Royals pinch-run specialist Terrance Gore," *The Kansas City Star*, October 9, 2014, http://www.kansascity.com/sports/mlb/kansas-city-royals/article2626436.html
• Andy McCullough, "Royals claim utility infielder Jayson Nix, activate Scott Downs from disabled list," *The Kansas City Star*, August 28, 2014, http://www.kansascity.com/sports/mlb/kansas-city-royals/article1319044.html
• Jeffrey Flanagan, "Royals' roster expansion includes one surprise: Eric Hosmer," FOX Sports Kansas City, September 1, 2014, http://www.foxsports.com/kansas-city/story/royals-roster-expansion-includes-one-surprise-eric-hosmer-090114
• Associated Press, "Torii Hunter fuels 6-run third as Detroit closes gap on K.C. to 1," ESPN.com, September 8, 2014, http://scores.espn.go.com/mlb/recap?id=340908106
• Associated Press, "Max Scherzer, Tigers close gap between Royals," ESPN.com, September 9, 2014, http://scores.espn.go.com/mlb/recap?id=340909106
• Associated Press, "Royals shut out Tigers for 1-game lead as James Shields deals gem," ESPN.com, Sept 10, 2014, http://scores.espn.go.com/mlb/recap?id=340910106
• Associated Press, "Lorenzo Cain's 3-run homer helps Royals close gap in Central race," ESPN.com, Sept 17, 2014, http://scores.espn.go.com/mlb/recap?id=340917107
• ESPN.com news services, "Brewers win Norichika Aoki bid rights," ESPN.com, December 19, 2011, http://espn.go.com/mlb/story/_/id/7365232/milwaukee-brewers-claim-rights-sign-japan-star-norichika-aoki
• Dick Kaegel, "Royals acquire Aoki from Brewers for Smith," MLB.com, December 5, 2013, http://m.mlb.com/news/article/64412590/
• Andy McCullough, "Despite falling short of expectations, Nori Aoki hangs on to spot in Royals' lineup," *The Kansas City Star*, June 5, 2014, http://www.kansascity.com/sports/mlb/kansas-city-royals/article470886/Despite-falling-short-of-expectations-Nori-Aoki-hangs-on-to-spot-in-Royals%E2%80%99-lineup.html
• "Royals Broadcasters," Kansas City Royals, 2015, http://kansascity.royals.mlb.com/team/broadcasters.jsp?c_id=kc

• Associated Press, "Tigers escape late jam to increase lead over Royals to 2½ games," ESPN.com, September 20, 2014, http://scores.espn.go.com/mlb/recap?id=340920107

• Associated Press, "Aoki, Guthrie, Royals avoid sweep, beat Tigers," ESPN.com, September 21, 2014, http://scores.espn.go.com/mlb/recap?id=340921107

• Associated Press, "Royals beat Indians, pull within 1 game of division-leading Detroit," ESPN.com, September 22, 2014, http://scores.espn.go.com/mlb/recap?gameId=340922105

• ESPN.com news services, "Jeremy Guthrie leads Royals past White Sox, to postseason berth," ESPN.com, September 26, 2014, http://scores.espn.go.com/mlb/recap?id=340926104

• Associated Press, "Royals miss shot at 1st placed in AL Central with loss to White Sox," ESPN.com, Sept 27, 2014, http://scores.espn.go.com/mlb/recap?id=340927104

• Associated Press, "Royals rally for 6-4 victory over White Sox," ESPN.com, September 28, 2014, http://scores.espn.go.com/mlb/recap?id=340928104

Chapter 10

• Brenden Kennedy, "Kansas City Royals leave Blue Jays with baseball's longest playoff drought," *Toronto Star*, September 28, 2014, http://www.thestar.com/sports/bluejays/2014/09/28/kansas_city_royals_leave_blue_jays_with_baseballs_longest_playoff_drought.html

• Mark Townsend, "Royals clinch first playoff since 1985, ending longest postseason drought in four major sports," Yahoo Sports, September 26, 2014, http://sports.yahoo.com/blogs/mlb-big-league-stew/royals-clinch-first-playoff-since-1985--ending-longest-postseason-drought-in-mlb-014824577.html

• Alan Van Zandt, "Local Bar Happy To Welcome Royals Fans For Wildcard Game," StJoeChannel.com, September 30, 2014, http://www.stjoechannel.com/story/d/story/local-bar-happy-to-welcome-royals-fans-for-wildcar/34371/-1qseHPEE0yAKXCJ2bk-yg

• Elle Moxley, "Royals Fans Rally in Anticipation of Wild Card Game," KCUR.org, Sept 29, 2014, http://kcur.org/post/royals-fans-rally-anticipation-wild-card-game

• Bill Pollock, "Royals will face Oakland in the one-game American League Wild Card, Tuesday night at Kauffman Stadium. Rally planned for Monday," Missourinet, September 28, 2014, http://www.missourinet.com/2014/09/28/royals-will-face-either-oakland-or-seattle-in-the-one-game-american-league-wild-card-game-will-be-played-tuesday-night-at-kauffman-stadium-rally-planned-for-monday/

• "MLB Team Stats – 2014," ESPN.com, http://espn.go.com/mlb/stats/team/_/stat/batting/league/al

• Jerry Crasnick, "Dayton Moore's vision validated," ESPN.com, September 30, 2014, http://espn.go.com/mlb/playoffs/2014/story/_/id/11617063/dayton-moore-vision-kansas-royals-validated

• Aaron Leibowitz, "A's-Royals Wild Card Game: Did you know?" MLB.com, September 28, 2014, http://m.mlb.com/news/article/96931988/as-royals-wild-card-game-did-you-know

• Doug Miller, "Streak to AL pennant defined 2014 for Royals," MLB.com, December 25, 2014, http://m.royals.mlb.com/news/article/104674896/streak-to-al-pennant-world-series-defined-2014-for-kc-royals

• David Coleman, "Athletics-Royals AL Wild Card time, TV, and online viewing information," SB Nation, September 30, 2014, http://www.crawfishboxes.com/2014/9/30/6872475/athletics-royals-al-wild-card-time-tv-and-online-viewing-information

• Kathleen Gier, "Royals go local for national anthem, first pitch," *The Kansas City Star*, September 30, 2014, http://www.kansascity.com/sports/mlb/kansas-city-royals/article2365170.html

• "A capsule look at the A's-Royals playoff game," *USA Today*, September 29, 2014, http://www.usatoday.com/story/sports/mlb/2014/09/29/a-capsule-look-at-the-as-royals-playoff-game/16457975/

• Associated Press, "Royals eliminate A's on Salvador Perez's walk-off single in 12th," ESPN.com, September 30, 2014, http://scores.espn.go.com/mlb/recap?gameId=340930107

Chapter 11

• "MLB Team Stats – 2014," ESPN.com, http://espn.go.com/mlb/stats/team/_/stat/batting/league/al/type/expanded

• Matt Snyder, "Royals-Angels ALDS preview: Who has the edge?" CBSSports.com, October 1, 2014, http://www.cbssports.com/mlb/eye-on-baseball/24733074/royals-angels-alds-preview-who-has-the-edge

• Greg Beacham, "Royals-Angels Preview," Yahoo Sports, October 1, 2014, http://sports.yahoo.com/news/royals-angels-preview-002235089--mlb.html

• "MLB Salaries 2014 Season," *USA Today*, http://www.usatoday.com/sports/mlb/salaries/2014/team/all/

• Anthony McCarron, "Game 1 ALDS opponents, Royals' Jason Vargas and Angels' Jered Weaver, planning family vacation together," *New York Daily News*, October 2, 2014, http://www.nydailynews.com/sports/baseball/royals-vargas-angels-weaver-vacation-alds-showdown-article-1.1961149

• Associated Press, "Mike Moustakas' HR in 11th sends Royals past Angels in ALDS opener," ESPN.com, October 2, 2014, http://scores.espn.go.com/mlb/recap?gameId=341002103

• Blair Kerkhoff, "Greg Holland's 2,000-mile trip to the mound," *The Kansas City Star*, October 3, 2014, http://www.kansascity.com/sports/mlb/kansas-city-royals/article2504911.html

• Associated Press, "Eric Hosmer's 2-run HR gives K.C. another extra-inning win, series lead," ESPN.com, October 3, 2014, http://scores.espn.go.com/mlb/recap?gameId=341003103
• Jim Caple, "Royals loving the late-inning drama," ESPN.com, October 4, 2014, http://espn.go.com/mlb/playoffs/2014/story/_/id/11638096/kansas-city-royals-loving-late-inning-drama
• Jorge L. Ortiz, "Albert Pujols hopes for happy homecoming in Kansas City," *USA Today*, Oct 5, 2014, http://www.usatoday.com/story/sports/mlb/2014/10/05/albert-pujols-kansas-city-home-angels-royals-playoffs/16734947/
• Arne Christensen, "Albert Pujols: revisiting the early years," The Hardball Times, June 15, 2010, http://www.hardballtimes.com/albert-pujols-revisiting-the-early-years/
• Associated Press, "Royals claim ALCS berth with sweep of regular-season-best Angels," ESPN.com, Oct 5, 2014, http://espn.go.com/mlb/recap?gameId=341005107
• Jim Caple, "Royals' sweep worth the wait," ESPN.com, October 6, 2014, http://espn.go.com/mlb/playoffs/2014/story/_/id/11649536/mlb-royals-sweep-angels-worth-wait
• Jaime Uribarri, "Royals players party with fans after sweeping Angels in ALDS," *New York Daily News*, October 6, 2014, http://www.nydailynews.com/sports/baseball/royals-players-party-fans-sweeping-angels-alds-article-1.1965212

Chapter 12
• Matt Snyder, "Orioles clinch American League East championship," CBSSports.com, September 16, 2014, http://www.cbssports.com/mlb/eye-on-baseball/24712390/orioles-clinch-american-league-east-championship
• "MLB Team Stats – 2014," ESPN.com, http://espn.go.com/mlb/stats/team/_/stat/batting
• Anthony Riccobono, "Orioles – Royals 2014: ALCS Prediction, Preview, Betting Odds For World Series, *International Business Times*, October 7, 2014, http://www.ibtimes.com/orioles-royals-2014-alcs-prediction-preview-betting-odds-world-series-1700773
• Ben Lindbergh, "2014 ALCS Preview: Royals vs. Orioles," Grantland, Oct 9, 2014, http://grantland.com/the-triangle/2014-mlb-playoffs-alcs-preview-royals-vs-orioles/
• Max Rieper and Kevin Ruprecht, "Orioles Series Preview: the American League Championship Series," Royals Review, October 10, 2014, http://www.royalsreview.com/2014/10/10/6951279/orioles-series-preview-the-american-league-championship-series
• STATS LLC, "Kansas City at Baltimore," CBSSports.com, October 10, 2014, http://www.cbssports.com/mlb/gametracker/preview/MLB_20141010_KC@BAL/royals-orioles-preview
• Associated Press, "Alex Gordon helps Royals prevail in extras again to open ALCS," ESPN.com, Oct 10, 2014, http://scores.espn.go.com/mlb/recap?gameId=341010101

• Sam Miller, "Playoff Prospectus," Baseball Prospectus, October 21, 2014, http://www.baseballprospectus.com/article.php?articleid=24885
• Blair Kerkhoff, "Royals are piling up postseason victories and babies," *The Kansas City Star*, October 9, 2014, http://www.kansascity.com/sports/mlb/kansas-city-royals/article2635811.html
• Dave Skretta, "ALCS rainout means Royals, Orioles aces could go Game 4," *The Detroit News*, October 13, 2014, http://www.detroitnews.com/story/sports/mlb/tigers/2014/10/13/rain-postpones-royals-orioles-game-alcs/17213051/
• Jerry Crasnick, "Jarrod Dyson: O's almost out of fight," ESPN.com, October 14, 2014, http://espn.go.com/mlb/playoffs/2014/story/_/id/11690369/2014-alcs-jarrod-dyson-kansas-city-royals-says-team-close-taking-fight-orioles
• Associated Press, "Royals edge Orioles to move within 1 win of World Series berth," ESPN.com, Oct 14, 2014, http://scores.espn.go.com/mlb/recap?gameId=341014107
• STATS LLC, "Orioles-Royals Preview," ESPN.com, October 15, 2014, http://scores.espn.go.com/mlb/preview?gameId=341015107
• Associated Press, "Royals hold off Orioles to complete sweep, advance to World Series," ESPN.com, October 15, 2014, http://scores.espn.go.com/mlb/recap?gameId=341015107
• Vahe Gregorian, "Royals' Holland stays true to roots after improbable rise," *The Kansas City Star*, June 3, 2014, http://www.kansascity.com/sports/spt-columns-blogs/vahe-gregorian/article445083/Royals%E2%80%99-Holland-stays-true-to-roots-after-improbable-rise.html
• Jim Caple, "Enjoy the moment, Royals fans!" ESPN.com, October 16, 2014, http://espn.go.com/mlb/playoffs/2014/story/_/id/11708900/enjoy-moment-kansas-city-royals-fans
• Jerry Crasnick, "Royals basking in glow of success," ESPN.com, October 16, 2014, http://espn.go.com/mlb/playoffs/2014/story/_/id/11708914/kansas-city-royals-basking-glow-success

Chapter 13

• Thomas Boswell, "The anomaly that is the Kansas City Royals in the World Series," *The Washington Post*, October 26, 2014, http://www.washingtonpost.com/sports/nationals/thomas-boswell-the-anomaly-that-is-the-kansas-city-royals-in-the-world-series/2014/10/26/9b35bc6e-5bdb-11e4-8264-deed989ae9a2_story.html
• Jim Caple, "Enjoy the moment, Royals fans!" ESPN.com, October 16, 2014, http://espn.go.com/mlb/playoffs/2014/story/_/id/11708900/enjoy-moment-kansas-city-royals-fans
• Jerry Crasnick, "Royals basking in glow of success," ESPN.com, October 16, 2014, http://espn.go.com/mlb/playoffs/2014/story/_/id/11708914/kansas-city-royals-basking-glow-success

• Bobby Bonett, "Kansas City Royals win AL pennant; postgame reaction from SiriusXM Sports," SiriusXM, October 16, 2014, http://blog.siriusxm.com/2014/10/16/kansas-city-royals-win-al-pennant-postgame-reaction-from-siriusxm-sports/
• "MLB Team Stats – 2014" ESPN.com, http://espn.go.com/mlb/stats/team/_/stat/batting/league/nl/sort/avg/order/true
• "MLB Salaries 2014 Season," *USA Today*, http://www.usatoday.com/sports/mlb/salaries/2014/team/all/
• SI Wire, "Royals slight betting favorites to win World Series over Giants," *Sports Illustrated*, October 17, 2014, http://www.si.com/mlb/2014/10/17/world-series-betting-odds-royals-vs-giants
• Jesse Spector, "World Series 2014 preview: Five keys to the Fall Classic for Giants, Royals," *Sporting News*, October 21, 2014, http://www.sportingnews.com/mlb/story/2014-10-20/world-series-2014-preview-prediction-giants-royals-odds-bullpen-stolen-bases-pablo-sandoval-billy-butler-brandon-belt
• "World Series national anthem performers and first pitch tossers," *Newsday*, October 29, 2014, http://www.newsday.com/sports/baseball/world-series-national-anthem-performers-and-first-pitch-tossers-1.9530422
• Associated Press, "Madison Bumgarner-led Giants put Royals' streak on ice for 1-0 lead," ESPN.com, October 21, 2014, http://scores.espn.go.com/mlb/recap?gameId=341021107
• Matt Bonesteel, "Why is Dodgers fan Rob Lowe taunting the Royals on Twitter during the World Series," *The Washington Post*, October 22, 2014, http://www.washingtonpost.com/blogs/early-lead/wp/2014/10/22/why-is-dodgers-fan-rob-lowe-taunting-the-royals-on-twitter-during-the-world-series/
• Pete Grathoff, "Baseball throws its support behind causes at the World Series," *The Kansas City Star*, October 21, 2014, http://www.kansascity.com/sports/mlb/kansas-city-royals/article3216586.html
• Associated Press, "Royals use 5-run 6th inning to roar past Giants, even World Series," ESPN.com, October 22, 2014, http://scores.espn.go.com/mlb/recap?gameId=341022107
• Tim Keown, "Hunter Pence: Sign-inspirer," *ESPN The Magazine*, December 4, 2014, http://espn.go.com/mlb/story/_/id/11972381/hunter-pence-talks-hunter-pence-signs-interview-issue
• Rick Chandler, "Royals Fan Comes Up With Possibly Greatest Hunter Pence Sign So Far," SportsGrid, October 22, 2014, http://www.sportsgrid.com/mlb/royals-fan-comes-up-with-possibly-greatest-hunter-pence-sign-so-far/
• Jayson Stark, "Yost wins chess match over Bochy," ESPN.com, October 23, 2014, http://espn.go.com/mlb/playoffs/2014/story/_/id/11748631/mlb-ned-yost-wins-chess-match-bruce-bochy

• Associated Press, "Eric Hosmer's sixth-inning RBI gives Royals 2-1 World Series lead," ESPN.com, October 24, 2014, http://scores.espn.go.com/mlb/recap?gameId=341024126

• Jim Caple, "Hunter Pence signs get a K.C. flavor," ESPN.com, October 25, 2014, http://espn.go.com/mlb/playoffs/2014/story/_/id/11758926/mlb-hunter-pence-signs-get-kansas-city-flavor

• Keith Jarrett, "An October to remember for Greg Holland," *Asheville Citizen-Times*, October 18, 2014, http://www.citizen-times.com/story/sports/2014/10/18/october-remember-greg-holland/17499337/

• Jayson Stark, "Ned Yost keeps managing to win," ESPN.com, October 26, 2014, http://espn.go.com/mlb/playoffs/2014/story/_/id/11759055/mlb-royals-ned-yost-keeps-managing-win

• Jerry Crasnick, "Giants stick with Ryan Vogelsong," ESPN.com, October 25, 2014, http://espn.go.com/mlb/playoffs/2014/story/_/id/11758373/mlb-giants-stick-ryan-vogelsong

• Associated Press, "Giants rally from 3-run deficit, surge past Royals to even World Series," ESPN.com, Oct 25, 2014, http://scores.espn.go.com/mlb/recap?id=341025126

• Associated Press, "Madison Bumgarner tosses 4-hit shutout to put Giants up 3-2," ESPN.com, October 26, 2014, http://scores.espn.go.com/mlb/recap?id=341026126

• Jerry Crasnick, "Royals retreat to familiar territory," ESPN.com, October 27, 2014, http://espn.go.com/mlb/playoffs/2014/story/_/id/11771592/mlb-royals-retreat-familiar-territory

• Associated Press, "Royals crush Giants to tie up World Series, force Game 7," ESPN.com, Oct 28, 2014, http://scores.espn.go.com/mlb/recap?gameId=341028107

• Associated Press, "Madison Bumgarner, Giants hold off Royals to win World Series," ESPN.com, Oct 29, 2014, http://scores.espn.go.com/mlb/recap?id=341029107

Chapter 14

• Jerry Crasnick, "Spirited Royals exit World Series," ESPN.com, October 30, 2014, http://espn.go.com/mlb/playoffs/2014/story/_/id/11788475/mlb-spirited-royals-exit-world-series

• John Viril, "Kansas City Royals World Series Loss Just Doesn't Feel Right," KC Kingdom, October 30, 2014, http://kckingdom.com/2014/10/30/kansas-city-royals-world-series-loss-just-doesnt-feel-right/

• Dick Kaegel, "Royals' Gordon reflects on World Series dash," MLB.com, December 1, 2014, http://m.royals.mlb.com/news/article/102853880/royals-alex-gordon-reflects-on-world-series-dash

• "Pickett's Charge," History Net, 2015, http://www.historynet.com/picketts-charge-gettysburg

• Associated Press, "Madison Bumgarner, Giants hold off Royals to win World Series," ESPN.com, Oct 29, 2014, http://scores.espn.go.com/mlb/recap?id=341029107

• Associated Press, "Madison Bumgarner tosses 4-hit shutout to put Giants up 3-2," ESPN.com, October 26, 2014, http://scores.espn.go.com/mlb/recap?id=341026126

• Jayson Stark, "Madison Bumgarner saves the Giants," ESPN.com, October 30, 2014, http://espn.go.com/mlb/playoffs/2014/story/_/id/11788829/mlb-madison-bumgarner-saves-giants

• Pete Grathoff, "Gov. Sam Brownback: I would have sent Alex Gordon," *The Kansas City Star*," January 15, 2015, http://www.kansascity.com/sports/spt-columns-blogs/for-petes-sake/article6838089.html

• Mitch Stephens, "Foothill High remembers Brandon Crawford" *San Francisco Chronicle*, October 29, 2012, http://www.sfgate.com/preps/article/Foothill-High-remembers-Brandon-Crawford-3991812.php

• Matthew Leach, "Statcast: Dissecting Gordon's odds of scoring," MLB.com, October 31, 2014, http://m.mlb.com/news/article/100150646/statcast-dissecting-alex-gordons-odds-of-scoring-tying-run-in-ninth-inning-of-game-7

• Kevin Ruprecht, "Season in review: Catchers," Royals Review, January 28, 2015, http://www.royalsreview.com/2015/1/28/7926555/season-in-review-catchers-royals-salvador-perez-erik-kratz

• Peggy Breit, "Fans show gratitude to Royals for thrilling postseason ride," KMBC.com, October 30, 2014, http://www.kmbc.com/news/fans-show-gratitude-to-royals-for-thrilling-postseason-ride/29437708

• Doug Miller, "Royals captivate KC with rollicking World Series run," MLB.com, December 25, 2014, http://m.royals.mlb.com/news/article/104899820/royals-captivated-kc-with-rollicking-world-series-run

• Joe Posnanski, "This team." HardballTalk, October 16, 2014, http://hardballtalk.nbcsports.com/2014/10/16/this-team/

• Jerry Crasnick, "Royals basking in glow of success," ESPN.com, October 16, 2014, http://espn.go.com/mlb/playoffs/2014/story/_/id/11708914/kansas-city-royals-basking-glow-success

• Andy McCullough, "Where the money went: Royals' opening-day payroll for 2014 vs. 2015," *The Kansas City Star*, December 17, 2014, http://www.kansascity.com/sports/spt-columns-blogs/ball-star/article4559452.html

Among the sources consulted for this book, I am especially appreciative of Baseball-Reference.com and ESPN.com. The box scores, player stats, game-by-game schedules, play-by-play listings, and other baseball facts provided by these websites were vital to my research.

About the Author

Kent Krause writes content for online high school history courses and social studies textbooks. He holds bachelor's and master's degrees from Iowa State University, and a doctorate from the University of Nebraska-Lincoln. In addition to his four books, he has published articles in *Great Plains Quarterly* and *The International Journal of the History of Sport*. USA Book News selected his novel *The All-American*  *King* as a category finalist for the National Best Books 2009 Awards. Kent lives in Nebraska with his wife Jill.

Visit Kent online at: **kentkrause.com**

Printed in Great Britain
by Amazon.co.uk, Ltd.,
Marston Gate.